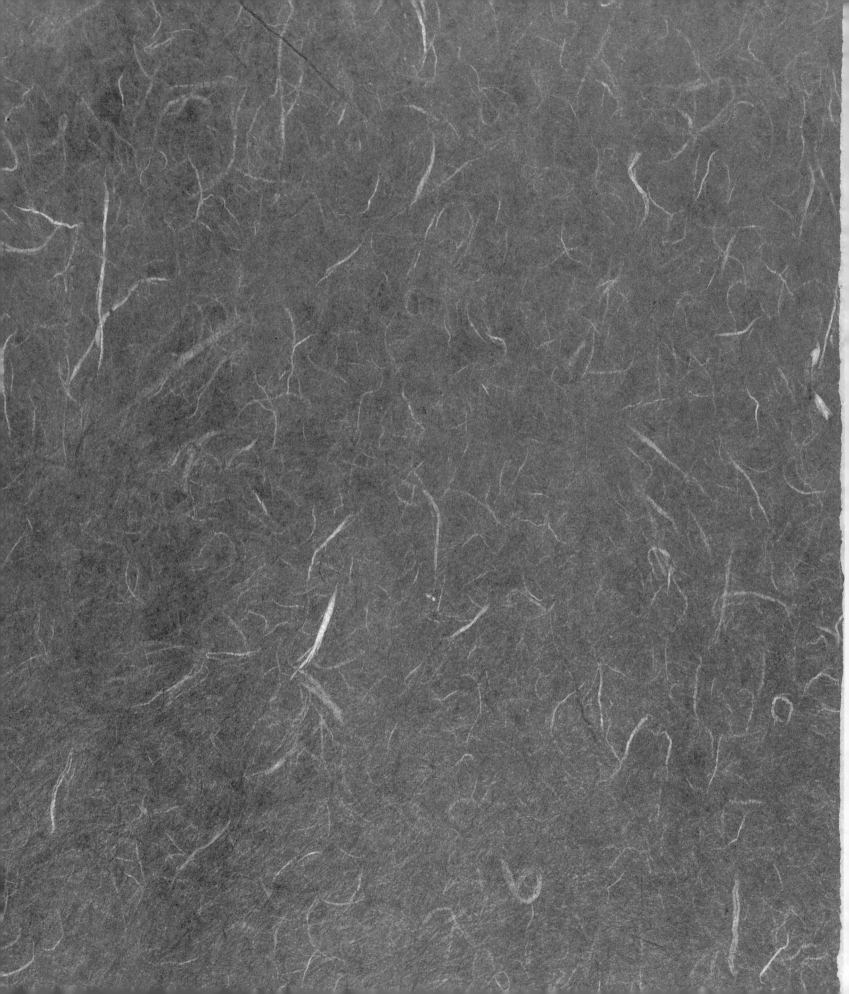

Great Women Chefs

Recipes on pages 169-73 © 1996 Jody Adams; pages 35-39 © 1996 Monique Barbeau; pages 95-99 © 1996 Lidia Bastianich,
page 97 from *La Cucina di Lidia* © 1990 by Lidia Bastianich, Doubleday; pages 65-69 © 1996 Catherine Brandel; pages 41-45
© 1996 Kathy Cary; pages 11-15 © 1996 Traci Des Jardins; pages 131-35 © 1996 Nancy Flume; pages 101-05 © 1996 Gale Gand;
pages 157-61 © 1996 Elka Gilmore; pages 125-29 © 1996 Joyce Goldstein; pages 53-57 © 1996 Deborah Hughes; pages 89-93
© 1996 Raji Jallepalli; pages 163-67 © 1996 Donna Katzl; pages 23-27 © 1996 Katy Keck; pages119-23 from *Cucina Simpatica*
© 1991 by Johanne Killeen and George Germon, reprinted by permission of HarperCollins Publishers, Inc.; pages144-49
© 1996 Mary Sue Milliken and Susan Feniger; pages 83-87 © 1996 Cindy Pawlcyn; pages 151-55 © 1996 Odessa Piper; pages 59-63
© 1996 Debra Ponzek; pages 17-21 © 1996 Nora Pouillon; pages 107-11 © 1996 Patty Queen; pages 29-33 © 1996 Teresa Rovito;
pages 137-41 © 1996 Anne Rosenzweig; pages 175-79 © 1996 RoxSand Scocos; pages 181-85 © 1996 Lindsey Shere; pages 113-17
© 1996 Peggy Smith; pages 71-75 © 1996 Susan Spicer; pages 47-51 © 1996 Sarah Stegner; pages 77-81 © 1996 Elizabeth Terry

Photo credits for chef photos: page 58 Tom Kirkman; page 70 Donn Young; page 82 Kirstie Laird;
page 100 Mitchell Canoff; page 150 Brent Nicastro; page 124 Richard Morgenstein; page 180 Robert Messick

Library of Congress Cataloging-in-Publication Data

Stillman, Julie.
Great women chefs : marvelous meals & innovative recipes from the stars of American cuisine/by Julie Stillman;
introduction by Alice Waters. — 1st ed.
p.   cm.
ISBN 1–57036–295–5 (alk. paper)
1. Cookery, American. 2. Menus. 3. Women cooks—United States.
I. Title.
TX715.S8575   1996
642'.4—dc20   96-15275
CIP

Published by Turner Publishing, Inc.
A Subsidiary of
Turner Broadcasting System, Inc.
1050 Techwood Drive, N.W.
Atlanta, Georgia 30318

Distributed by Andrews and McMeel
A Universal Press Syndicate Company
4900 Main Street
Kansas City, Missouri 64112

Developed and Produced by

Julie Stillman • Gary Chassman
Burlington, Vermont

Design • Eugenie Seidenberg Delaney

Food Photography • Len Mastri

Food Styling • Melissa McClelland

First Edition
10 9 8 7 6 5 4 3 2 1

Printed in China

Great Women Chefs

Marvelous Meals & Innovative Recipes from the Stars of American Cuisine

Julie Stillman

INTRODUCTION BY ALICE WATERS

FOOD PHOTOGRAPHY • LEN MASTRI
FOOD STYLING • MELISSA McCLELLAND

PRODUCED BY VERVE EDITIONS

Turner Publishing, Inc.
ATLANTA

Contents

$\mathcal{I}$ntroduction

ALICE WATERS

YOU HOLD IN YOUR HANDS a delightful treasury of recipes written by thirty remarkable women. Of course, there is nothing very new in that, for remarkable women cooks have been writing indispensable cookbooks for hundreds of years. However, each of the cooks who have contributed to this volume is a true chef—*a chief cook,* to quote the dictionary's definition of the word—and a book such as this one could not have been compiled until now, when many women have become, at last, the chief cooks of serious restaurants. Until quite recently, most women cooks have had to be content with being either housewife, domestic servant, or home economics teacher. A woman as chef of a fashionable restaurant would have been all but unthinkable. The Culinary Institute of America did not even admit women until 1970, and as late as 1985, only about 12 percent of its graduates were women. Today the number has climbed to about one third, and nowadays, thankfully, it is not so rare to find a women at the helm of a restaurant.

A kitchen, after all, is a natural place for a woman to be. In my restaurant kitchen, I like to have both men and women, with both kinds of energies represented, and all the dynamics between the two of them. But I have found that there is a difference between men and women in the kitchen. There is something women understand instinctively in a way that men, perhaps, do not: that food is primarily about nourishment. Cooking is more than an art; it is a daily sacrament in which we act out our commitment to each other, to society, and to the earth.

The thirty women here have all been chefs at celebrated restaurants. Each one is not only a culinary artist but a woman at the top of her profession, and each one shares with us some interesting recipes to cook and some interesting lessons to ponder over the many roads to professional success. Just as their recipes range from the familiar, comforting, and traditional to the daring, the curious, and the downright recherché, so do the biographical sketches of these wonderful women display the splendid variety of trajectories a woman's life can take when it is lived in the single-minded pursuit of excellence.

Some of these women chefs were practically born in the kitchen. Some plunged into kitchen work in their teens and now run the very kitchens where they were first hired. Others passed through arduous apprenticeships before they took command of the restaurants they have made famous, while others turned to the profession late in life and stepped on stage, as it were, completely prepared. Still others attended culinary schools, assisted in cooking classes, and were run ragged by the demands of catering businesses before they were able to mastermind their own restaurants. Before they became chefs, some of these women were engineers, photographers, artists, scientists, teachers, Wall Street financiers, and communards. If there is any common thread that runs through all their stories, it is that cliché from the biographies of all high achievers—that perseverance and unswerving dedication are ultimately rewarded.

The cuisine of these women is equally eclectic, and their recipes show off a far-reaching and insatiable curiosity. Anyone wishing to verify the enormous increase in sophistication and variety in the American professional kitchen need only open this book at random. Some of these cooks, inspired by their foremothers, are proud to resuscitate and keep alive the culinary traditions of their native places; many others, boldly combining influences from several continents, boast of their innovativeness: one cooks a fusion of Indian and French cuisine, still another calmly claims to draw from a core repertoire consisting of no fewer than seven cuisines: Asian, French, Italian, Spanish, Moroccan, Native American, and South American. However, almost half the women here acknowledge a more conservative reliance on the foundation of French, Italian, or, more vaguely, Mediterranean tradition. And even though the adventurous Mary Sue Milliken and Susan Feniger say that they love soaking up ideas from other cultures, they add, a little reassuringly, that they don't like mixing them up.

Most refreshingly, regardless of their leanings, fully half of the women in these pages say they draw their inspiration primarily from their finest and freshest local ingredients. A few are eloquent on the subject: Lidia Bastianich says, "Food for me is really the protagonist. . . .The product is 50 percent or more of what I do." Odessa Piper is perhaps the most radical purist of them all. Even though she is located in Madison, Wisconsin, she believes in serving only seasonal ingredients from what she calls her local "foodshed" (as in watershed); in the wintertime, by necessity, 50 percent of her menu is composed from ingredients she has preserved herself.

Occasionally in these pages you will hear echoes of the ingrained prejudice and condescension that has dogged the heels of many of the women who have been in the vanguard that opened up the profession. No one dwells on it, but there has long been an undercurrent of the most mindless and insulting sexism in the mostly male culinary establishment. Here you will read of the woman who was not allowed to approach the stove—the lowliest male apprentice took precedence—and of the woman who was told, when she applied for a job in an all-male kitchen, "It would create havoc to have a pretty young thing like you in my kitchen." (She was ultimately hired, and is silent about any havoc that may have ensued.)

But you will also read about Elizabeth Terry, who says, "When I go to the table, a lot of men pat me on the hand and say, 'Honey, you sure can cook!' I take it as a compliment, although other women might not." Who can blame her for preferring to do so? Like all artists, chefs don't especially want criticism—and particularly not constructive criticism. They prefer dazzled gratitude and extravagant praise. All the chefs in this book sure can cook, and I will bet they are not flattered enough. And truly, for them there is no such thing as too many compliments. They are astonishing. It is impossible to exaggerate the stamina, artistic vision, courage, and sheer good humor that it takes to run a restaurant if it is to be both an artistic and a financial success. I know from experience.

More than once as I read the stories of the women in this book and browsed through their recipes, I was reminded of the archetypical great woman chef, the heroine of "Babette's Feast," a small masterpiece of a short story by Isak Dinesen, first published in 1958, in a collection entitled *Anecdotes of Destiny*. It is a story all about reconciliation, and it demonstrates the great truth that, in this life, anything is possible.

In the story, set in a small provincial Norwegian town, two pious sisters, members of an extremely strict Lutheran sect founded by their father, take in a storm-tossed refugee who arrives at their doorstep after the suppression of the Paris Commune in 1870. Babette becomes the invaluable maid-of-all-work for the sisters, making it possible for them to be even more pious and charitable than ever. Twelve years pass. When Babette announces she has won ten thousand francs in the lottery, the sisters, assuming she will leave them, reluctantly grant her request that she be allowed to cook them a real French meal to celebrate the one hundredth birthday of their father. The guests include a distinguished visiting general who years before had been a handsome young cavalry officer in love with the elder sister. To the incomprehension of the brethren, but to the amazement of the general, the food and wines are the best in the world. Tongues are loosened, old scores are forgiven, and the bliss of Paradise descends on the party. After the guests have departed, the sisters go to the kitchen. No one has said a word about the food. "It was quite a nice dinner, Babette," they tell the exhausted chef. And then they learn what the reader has by now deduced: Babette is none other than the former chef of the fictional Café Anglais in Paris, the restaurant where years before, the general had tasted some of the incomparable dishes that have just been served. Babette had been the culinary genius of her age. The general has recalled being told that the chef has turned dinner at the Café Anglais ". . . into a kind of love affair—into a love affair of the noble and romantic category in which one no longer distinguishes between bodily and spiritual appetite or satiety!"

"I am a great artist," Babette now tells the sisters, and reveals that she has spent all her lottery winnings on the dinner. "No, I shall never be poor," she says, "A great artist, Mesdames, is never poor. We have something, Mesdames, of which other people know nothing." And then, quoting another artist, an opera singer who has figured in the story, she says. "'It is terrible and unbearable to an artist . . . to be encouraged to do, to be applauded for doing, his second best. . . .Through all the world there goes one long cry from the heart of the artist: Give me leave to do my utmost!'"

Thank heaven that we have finally given leave to so many women to do their utmost. Unlike Babette, the chefs in this volume are able to enchant us here on earth, instead of having to wait until they reach Paradise to enchant the angels. Their inspiring example—and their delicious recipes—should help anyone seeking to turn even a dinner at home into a noble love affair.

ALICE WATERS

About this book

The menus listed on the first page of each chapter are presented in the order that the chef intended the courses be served. Because of design considerations, occasionally it was necessary to present the recipes in a different order. The descriptions that accompany each recipe were provided by the chefs.

The wine suggestions given for each menu are from Irving Shelby Smith, and are intended for the main course. You will find additional selections for each meal in the Wine Notes on pages 186 and 187.

A special thanks to the thirty chefs who created the wonderful menus and recipes in this book, and shared their stories with me.

For their patience, encouragement, and general good humor, I am especially grateful to Kathy Buttler and Karen Smith of Turner Publishing, Frankie Whitman of the IAWCR, Cheryl Dorschner, Eugenie Delaney, and Jeff Nagle.

J. S.

Traci Des Jardins

DESPITE ITS STAR-STUDDED list of celebrity owners (Robin Williams, Robert De Niro, and Francis Ford Coppola) those who have eaten at Rubicon in San Francisco would agree that the real star is chef Traci Des Jardins.

Dedicated to a career in French cooking, her hands-on training includes four apprenticeships in France and more than ten years cooking at French restaurants in the U.S. At the age of seventeen Des Jardins went to work in the pantry at Joachim Splichal's Seventh Street Bistro in Los Angeles. Not yet twenty, she moved to Roanne, France, for an apprenticeship with the famous Troisgros family, who brought nouvelle cuisine to French cooking in the '60s. In 1987 she came to New York as sous-chef at Drew Nieporent's Montrachet, an affiliation that would presage her appointment as his executive chef at Rubicon. Following another stint with Splichal, this time at the acclaimed Patina in Los Angeles, Des Jardins finally settled in San Francisco in 1991 where she helped Elka Gilmore open her eponymous restaurant. Rubicon opened in 1994 with Des Jardins at the helm, and she was named the James Beard Rising Star Chef of the Year in 1995.

That's a lot to accomplish by the age of thirty, but perhaps it could be expected from someone whose first word was "eat." Des Jardins hails from the tiny town of Firebaugh in California's San Joaquin Valley. Food was important in her family and she remembers eating her Cajun grandfather's shrimp creole and her Mexican grandmother's fresh tortillas. Growing up in the rich farmlands of California instilled in her a lifelong passion for the bonanza of fresh produce in her native state.

Des Jardins' food could be described as contemporary French cuisine with an American accent. Her lunch menu may feature a portobello mushroom sandwich with aioli and grilled red onions, or crabcake with fennel-and-pepper ragoût. Dinner might begin with a sautéed foie gras with sunchokes and tamarind sauce, followed by John Dory with roasted Sonoma beets and a red-wine onion jus. For this menu Des Jardins has selected some of the most dynamic dishes in her repertoire.

Ahi Tuna with Chickpea Pancakes, Oven-Dried Tomatoes & Haricots Verts

Serves 8

2 pounds number-1 grade Ahi tuna cut into 1½-inch steaks	⅛ cup chopped fresh mint
Salt & freshly ground black pepper	⅛ cup chopped Italian parsley
3 tablespoons vegetable oil	1 cup chicken or vegetable stock
2 cups cooked chickpeas	½ cup oven-dried tomatoes (see recipe following)
½ cup extra virgin olive oil	¼ pound haricots verts, blanched
3 large eggs	1 teaspoon lemon zest
¼ cup all-purpose flour	1 tablespoon lemon juice
½ cup milk	

Season tuna with salt and pepper. Heat 2 tablespoons of vegetable oil in a large skillet over high heat. When very hot, sear the tuna for about 1 minute on each side. Place the tuna on a baking sheet and set aside.

In a food processor or blender, puree 1½ cups of the chickpeas with ¼ cup of the olive oil. In a large bowl, whisk together eggs, flour, and milk. Stir in the chickpea puree, mint, parsley, and salt and pepper to taste.

In a large skillet, heat remaining 1 tablespoon vegetable oil over medium-low heat. Drop batter onto skillet to make 3-inch pancakes. Cook until golden brown, about 3 minutes on each side. Keep warm on a platter.

To assemble: Preheat oven to 450° F. In a saucepan, bring stock to a boil, add oven-dried tomatoes and remaining ½ cup of the chickpeas and reduce heat to low. Add the remaining ¼ cup of the olive oil, haricots verts, lemon zest, and lemon juice. Mix well and season to taste with additional salt and pepper.

Heat the tuna for about 2 minutes, until just warm, but still rare.

On a large platter or on individual plates, arrange the pancakes, tomato-chickpea mixture, and tuna.

Inspired by the flavors of the Mediterranean, this dish blends creamy chickpeas, fruity olive oil, tangy tomatoes, and rich tuna. With a little advance preparation, the final execution should be quite simple. If you make the oven-dried tomatoes and pancake batter a day in advance, finishing the dish will be a snap.

11

Oven-Dried Tomatoes

12 roma tomatoes, blanched and peeled
4   tablespoons extra virgin olive oil

2   sprigs fresh thyme
    Salt & freshly ground black pepper

Preheat oven to 200° F. Lightly oil a baking sheet.

Cut the outside "petals" from the tomatoes. (The cores may be saved for another use such as salsa or tomato sauce.)

Sprinkle the prepared baking sheet with thyme and salt and pepper to taste. Place the tomatoes on the baking sheet and bake for 2-3 hours, or until slightly "dried."

(These may stored in a tightly covered jar in the refrigerator for about 1 week.)

Seared Scallops with Artichoke & Arugula Salad

Serves 8

2   lemons
6   artichokes
3   tablespoons extra virgin olive oil
2   bunches arugula, washed and stemmed
1   shallot, peeled and diced

3   tablespoons finely minced chives
3   tablespoons balsamic vinegar
    Salt & freshly ground black pepper
18 large sea scallops, muscles removed
1   tablespoon canola oil
3   tablespoons unsalted butter

Squeeze juice of 2 lemons into a bowl of water (lemon water will keep artichokes from discoloring). Cut the tough outer leaves from artichokes and trim until only the heart remains; remove the fuzzy "choke." Slice artichoke hearts into ¼ inch slices.

In a large skillet, heat 1 tablespoon of the olive oil over medium heat. Sauté the artichokes until slightly golden and tender, about 7 minutes. Transfer to a bowl and keep warm.

In a large mixing bowl combine arugula, shallots, and chives. Whisk 1 tablespoon of the balsamic vinegar with the remaining 2 tablespoons of the olive oil, and salt and pepper to taste. Set aside.

Season scallops with salt and pepper. In the skillet, heat canola oil over medium-high heat; sear the scallops about 1½ - 2 minutes on each side, depending on the size. Transfer to a platter and keep warm. Add the warm artichokes to the arugula and dress with balsamic vinaigrette, season with salt and pepper to taste, toss well.

In a sauté pan, heat butter over medium-high heat until golden brown. Let cool for about 1 minute and add the remaining 2 tablespoons of the balsamic vinegar, salt, and pepper.

Place the scallops around the salad and drizzle the brown-butter vinaigrette over them.

Although the process of "turning" an artichoke is at first a daunting task, once you get the hang of it, you will find the results both delicious and quite unusual. The natural nuttiness of the artichoke and the silky texture of the scallops combine beautifully with the spicy arugula. The easy and satisfying brown-butter vinaigrette ties the whole dish together.

cs

Muscovy Duck Breast with Turnips, Tatsoi, Pears & Honey-Coriander Sauce

Serves 8

¼ cup coriander seeds, plus
 1 tablespoon, toasted
4 tablespoons unsalted butter
3 bunches baby turnips, peeled,
 cleaned, and quartered, about 2 cups
½ cup chicken stock
6 Asian pears
1 lemon, juiced
½ cup sugar
¼ pound fresh ginger, peeled and
 chopped coarsely

¾ cup honey
¼ cup sherry wine vinegar
1 bunch cilantro, washed
2 cups reduced duck stock (optional)
8 small Muscovy duck breasts, boned
 and trimmed
 Salt & freshly ground black pepper
4 cups baby tatsoi, washed and dried
 (may substitute spinach)

I developed this dish for Rubicon, but its original inspiration comes from a great French chef I worked with in Paris. I've adapted my recipe to use American ingredients and less complicated techniques.

℘

In a sauté pan, toast 1 tablespoon of the coriander seeds over medium heat, until they give off a toasty aroma. (Be careful not to burn.) Let them cool, and crush lightly with a mortar and pestle.

To make turnips: In a large sauté pan, melt butter over medium-high heat. Add turnips and sweat for 1 minute. Add chicken stock, reduce the heat and simmer slowly until the turnips are tender, about 5 minutes. Set aside in the pan, reserving the cooking liquid.

To make pears: Peel, core, and quarter the pears. Cover with water and lemon juice and set aside. Place sugar in a large stainless steel saucepan, add about ¼ cup water to moisten, and cook over medium-high heat, stirring occasionally, until the sugar becomes a golden brown color, about 5-7 minutes. Stir in half of the ginger, about 3 tablespoons water, and pears. Cook until slightly caramelized but still crisp in the center, about 10 minutes. Transfer to a platter to keep warm.

To make sauce: Place honey in a medium-sized stainless steel saucepan; cook over medium-high heat until the honey begins to caramelize, about 5 minutes. Add the remaining ginger and ¼ cup of the coriander seeds. Cook until the coriander is fragrant, about 3 minutes. Add vinegar and cilantro and simmer until the vinegar is reduced by one half. Add reduced duck stock, if using, and reduce further until slightly thick, about 5 minutes. (If desired, the duck stock may be omitted and the honey-caramel sauce may be used as a simple glaze for the duck breasts rather than an actual sauce.) When the sauce is of the desired consistency, strain through a fine strainer and keep warm.

To prepare duck: Preheat oven to 450° F. Season duck breasts with salt and pepper on both sides. Heat a large, heavy-bottomed, ovenproof skillet to medium-high, and place duck skin-side down in

(continued on next page)

(Muscovy Duck Breast continued)

the skillet. Cook over medium to medium-high heat, slowly rendering the fat until skin is crispy and deep golden brown, about 5 minutes. Place in oven for about 5 minutes or until medium rare. Remove from oven, cover, and keep warm.

To assemble: Reheat the turnips in the cooking liquid. Add tatsoi and cook until slightly wilted, about 1 minute. Place the turnips, tatsoi, and pears on a platter or on individual plates, slice the duck breasts and fan on top. Spoon the sauce or glaze over the dish. Garnish with the toasted, crushed coriander seeds.

pple Tarts

Serves 12

1 pound puff pastry dough
1 egg yolk
¼ cup apricot jam
4 ounces almond paste or marzipan

9 Granny Smith apples or other tart, crisp, baking apples, peeled and cored
¼ cup fresh lemon juice
¾ cup sugar for baking

Preheat oven to 400° F.

Roll puff pastry dough to a thickness of ¼ inch. (The store-bought variety will most likely already be this thickness.) With a cookie cutter, cut dough into twelve 5-inch circles. With a fork, poke a few holes in the dough.

Whisk together the egg yolk with 2 teaspoons of water. Brush over the pastry rounds, covering completely. Spread a very thin layer of jam over each tart. Roll approximately 1 teaspoon almond paste

into a ball. Repeat with the rest of the paste. Flatten each ball like a coin and place in center of each tart shell.

Slice apples very thinly with a knife or mandoline. Arrange slices around each tart, using about ¾ of each apple per tart. Brush with lemon juice. Sprinkle each tart generously with sugar and bake for 10-15 minutes, or until bottoms are golden brown. Dust with confectioners' sugar and serve with Green-Apple Ice and a little crème fraîche.

Green-Apple Ice

½ cup sugar
¼ cup water
2 cups fresh apple juice

3 tablespoons fresh lemon juice
2 tablespoons Calvados

In a medium-sized saucepan, combine sugar and water over high heat, bring to a boil, stirring until sugar is dissolved, about 10 minutes.

Juice apples with peels on through a juicer. (This helps keep the color of the ice green.) Stir syrup into apple juice, and add lemon juice and Calvados. Pour into a shallow, nonaluminum baking dish and

freeze. When ice is half frozen, scrape with a fork to break up the ice crystals. Return to freezer until set. To serve, scrape ice out with a spoon or ice cream scoop. (Or freeze in an ice cream maker according to manufacturer's instructions.) *(Ice may be made up to 3 days ahead and stored in a tightly covered container in the freezer.)*

This recipe was developed by my pastry chef, Elizabeth Falkner, as we sought the perfect apple tarts. They are one of my favorite desserts— I make a habit of sampling them wherever I find them—and I think that Elizabeth has developed a truly formidable tart. Just a note on the puff pastry: There are many excellent commercial ones; choose one with all butter.

&

Nora Pouillon

An Elegant Spring Dinner

◆

Sautéed Morels
with
Goat Cheese, Spinach
& Beet Vinaigrette

Grilled
Maine Salmon
in
Lemongrass Broth

Baby Lettuce
with
Edible Flowers &
Raspberry Vinaigrette

Strawberry Shortcake
with
Light Whipped Cream

BLANC DE NOIRS
Maison Deutz
or
Mumm Napa Valley

WASHINGTON HAS BECOME a dining capital as well as the political hub of the United States and Nora Pouillon is one of the reasons. Among the pioneers in popularizing organic food, she is truly one of D.C.'s power chefs. Her "biodynamic cuisine" means using the freshest ingredients. She works closely with local purveyors to assure that the food she begins with is without chemicals, additives, or pesticides. Although this adds untold time and expense on her part, the results are well worth it. The elegant multiethnic food that is the hallmark of Restaurant Nora is considered to be among Washington's best.

Even though she was born in Vienna, Pouillon did not grow up with the stereotypical Austrian fare: fried foods and whipped cream. The simply prepared, wholesome food cooked by her parents inspired her lifelong commitment to healthy cooking.

She moved to Washington in the mid-'60s, and in 1973 started a cooking school called The Low-Budget Gourmet. Restaurant Nora opened in 1979, and attracted a loyal following. It is only recently, however, that Pouillon has received the same notice that some of her more famous colleagues have enjoyed for years—as artistic and health-conscious food has become important (and fashionable) on the East Coast.

A member of Washington's Les Dames D'Escoffier, a group that promotes women in the food business, Pouillon attributes the greater visibility of women chefs today to women learning how to network and promote themselves on the culinary circuit—something their male counterparts have been doing successfully for decades.

On the back of each menu at Nora, Pouillon elaborates on the ingredients she uses: pork raised in the Blue Mountains of Pennsylvania and then cured at the restaurant; farm-raised trout smoked with applewood; fresh goat cheese and local produce from small farms.

Each of her dishes is seasonally inspired and bursting with flavor. This beautiful springtime meal is a stunning example of the innovative, fresh cuisine that has become Nora Pouillon's trademark.

16

Sautéed Morels with Goat Cheese, Spinach & Beet Vinaigrette

Serves 4

VINAIGRETTE

  4 large shallots, peeled
  1 teaspoon olive oil
     Sea salt & freshly ground black pepper
  4 small beets (about 4 ounces each), greens trimmed
  ⅛ teaspoon caraway seeds
  1 tablespoon red wine vinegar
  ¼ cup canola oil

MORELS

  ½ pound morel mushrooms, washed and dried
  1 tablespoon olive oil
  2 tablespoons minced shallots
  2 tablespoons minced garlic
     Sea salt & freshly ground black pepper
1½-2 tablespoons sherry, white wine, or balsamic vinegar
  6 ounces spinach, washed, stemmed, and dried
  4 ounces goat cheese, cut in ¼-inch cubes

To make vinaigrette: Preheat oven to 400° F. Place shallots in a small non-reactive baking dish. Dress with olive oil and season with salt and pepper to taste. Cover with aluminum foil and bake for 30-40 minutes or until soft.

In a small saucepan steam or boil beets for 15-20 minutes. Peel the beets while still warm and put them in a blender with the roasted shallots, caraway seeds, salt, pepper, vinegar, and just enough water to cover the blades (about ½ cup).

Puree, and with the machine running, add canola oil in a thin stream, blending until emulsified. Add an additional ¼ cup water, if necessary, to thin the vinaigrette to the consistency of heavy cream.

To make morels: Wash mushrooms quickly, immersing them in cold water and draining them on kitchen or paper

(continued next page)

Morels are honeycombed, cone-shaped mushrooms that belong to the same family as the truffle. Their earthy and nutty flavor is a springtime delicacy. Paired with spinach and a crimson vinaigrette, these mushrooms make a beautiful first course.

(Sautéed Morels continued)

towels. Do not let them become water-logged. Set aside.

In a medium-sized sauté pan, heat olive oil. Add shallots and garlic and sauté for 2-3 minutes. Lower the heat, add the morels and continue sautéing, stirring from time to time, until the morels are softened, about 3 minutes. Season with salt and pepper to taste. Add vinegar, raise the heat and cook until most of the liquid has evaporated, about 2 more minutes. Stir in spinach and sauté briefly, just until wilted. Remove from the heat.

To assemble: Divide the beet vinaigrette among 4 luncheon-sized plates. Arrange the morel mixture on top of the vinaigrette. Garnish each plate with several goat-cheese cubes and serve warm.

Grilled Maine Salmon in Lemongrass Broth

Serves 4

4 ounces Pad Thai noodles or rice sticks

1 3-inch piece of fresh ginger, peeled and sliced

1 stalk lemongrass, outer leaves removed and thinly sliced

1-2 jalapeño chilies to taste, sliced

1 cup dry sherry (optional)

2 tablespoons Nuoc Nam or Thai fish sauce, to taste

2 large carrots, peeled and thinly sliced

16 shiitake mushrooms, washed, stemmed, and quartered

4 scallions, trimmed and sliced thinly on the diagonal

4 salmon fillets, about 6 ounces each, skinned

1 teaspoon canola oil

4 ounces tatsoi or watercress, stems trimmed

½ cup fresh cilantro leaves

Preheat the grill or broiler. Soak Pad Thai noodles or rice sticks in hot water until softened, about 3 minutes. Drain and set aside.

Place ginger, lemongrass, and chilies in a small chopper and process until minced, or mince finely by hand.

In a medium saucepan over high heat, bring 6 cups water or 5 cups water and 1 cup dry sherry to a boil. Add ginger mixture. Season with Nuoc Nam. Add carrots, shiitakes, scallions, and drained noodles or rice sticks. Reduce heat and simmer about 1 minute. *(The broth can be made ahead up to this point.)*

Brush salmon with canola oil and cook until the fish turns opaque and medium-rare, about 3 minutes on each side.

Just before serving, stir tatsoi or watercress into broth. Ladle the broth into 4 large soup bowls, dividing the vegetables evenly. Top with salmon and garnish with cilantro.

This dish is an Asian fish soup elevated to an entrée by presenting the broth as a base for a lovely whole fillet of salmon. Be sure to look for fresh lemongrass—it has an unbelievable aroma and taste. You can also try this dish with scallops, shrimp, or crabmeat.

Baby Lettuce with Edible Flowers & Raspberry Vinaigrette

Serves 4

With its floral accent this salad is a feast for the eyes. Nasturtiums are one of the best-tasting flowers — they are peppery like watercress or radishes. If you can't find nasturtiums, use marigold or calendula petals.

ᔆ

VINAIGRETTE

3 ounces fresh raspberries
1 teaspoon fresh lemon juice
¼ cup orange juice
2 tablespoons canola oil
  Sea salt & freshly ground black
  pepper

SALAD

½ pound baby lettuce or mesclun mix,
  washed, dried, and torn
16 nasturtium flowers
8 pansies or 16 violas

To make vinaigrette: In a blender, puree the raspberries, lemon and orange juices, and canola oil until smooth and emulsified. Add salt and pepper to taste.

To make salad: Wash the flowers by floating them in a large basin of water.

Carefully spin or pat dry — they are delicate. Refrigerate until ready to use.

Toss lettuce with the raspberry vinaigrette. Divide among 4 luncheon-sized plates. Garnish with flowers and serve.

Strawberry Shortcake
with Light Whipped Cream

Serves 4

SHORTCAKE

1⅓ cups all-purpose flour
3 tablespoons sugar
1 tablespoon baking powder
¼ teaspoon salt
6 tablespoons cold unsalted butter, cut into ¼-inch dice
½ cup milk
1 teaspoon fresh lemon juice
½ teaspoon pure vanilla extract

STRAWBERRIES

2 pints strawberries, washed and hulled
2 tablespoons sugar
1 tablespoon Grand Marnier or orange juice

WHIPPED CREAM

2 egg whites
2 tablespoons powdered sugar
½ cup heavy cream
  Mint sprigs for garnish

To make shortcake: Preheat oven to 375° F. Line a medium-sized sheet pan with aluminum foil or parchment paper.

Place flour, 2 tablespoons of the sugar, baking powder, and salt in a medium-sized bowl. Add butter and work it between your fingers until the texture is like coarse crumbs. Or prepare the dough in a food processor: Use an on-off pulsing motion until the dough has consistency of coarse crumbs. Add milk, lemon juice, and vanilla and stir with a fork to blend. The dough will be very soft.

Using an ice cream scoop or a large spoon, scoop 4 portions of the dough onto the prepared baking sheet, spacing the scoops 1-2 inches apart. Flatten each scoop into a 3½-inch circle and sprinkle with the remaining tablespoon of sugar. Bake about 30 minutes, or until golden and firm on the outside.

To prepare strawberries: Cut strawberries into halves or quarters, depending on size. Toss with sugar and Grand Marnier or orange juice and set aside until the berries release some of their juices. Crush some of the berries with the back of a spoon to make the juices thicker.

To make whipped cream: Place egg whites in a medium-sized bowl, add sugar and whip by hand until the whites form firm, but not dry, peaks. In a small bowl, whip cream by hand until it forms soft peaks. Fold the cream into the beaten egg whites.

To assemble: Split the shortcakes horizontally. Place the bottom half of each shortcake on a luncheon-sized plate. Add some of the light whipped cream to each shortcake, then add the strawberries and top with the remaining cream. Cover with the top half of the shortcake, placing it at a slight angle. Repeat with the other 3 shortcakes. Garnish each with a sprig of fresh mint.

The freshest local berries and a fluffy whipped cream make this dessert favorite a special treat.

Katy Keck

W HEN I WAS FIVE YEARS OLD, my grandfather died, and I have a vivid memory of baking a 'sympathy cake' for my mother and grandmother in my Easy Bake Oven." Thus began Katy Keck's endeavors as a chef. But she did not take a direct route from the Easy Bake Oven to the industrial stove at New World Grill in midtown Manhattan where she is co-owner and executive chef. Cooking became a career option only after she earned an M.B.A. and took a seven-year detour on Wall Street in the '80s. "I've found that (business) background to be so helpful in restaurant management, because a restaurant really is a small business before it's a restaurant. In addition to having food on the table you have to be an accountant and a marketer and a banker and a plumber, mother, and nurse as well," Keck observes.

In 1986, while Keck was putting together a business plan for a retail food store and taking professional catering classes, a teacher encouraged her to enter a recipe contest. She won the grand prize for her Marie Brizard Chocolate Torte recipe. The prize: an apprenticeship at Le Grand Monarque in Chartres, France. After a week in France, she wrote to her company on Wall Street and said she wouldn't be coming back. She followed the apprenticeship with a year of internships in three Michelin-starred restaurants. "It was the highlight year of my life—at thirty-one, I was old enough to know what I wanted out of the experience. Although I was miserable working for some of the men in France, I knew it was what I needed to do. I wasn't easily intimidated. Being female and American, people had no expectations of me, so it was very hard to disappoint them!"

Keck subsequently worked as a food consultant doing food styling, recipe development and testing, marketing, and coordinating special events. In 1993 she opened New World Grill with partner Richard Barber.

Keck describes her food as contemporary American with Asian and Southwestern influences. In an effort to present healthier choices for restaurant patrons she uses quicker and lighter cooking techniques than the classic French. She chose pork as the main dish for this meal because she thinks it's an important, often ignored, ingredient in low-fat cooking. This festive menu showcases Katy Keck's bold style, offering a riot of color and flavor, and a truly unique bread pudding.

Shrimp-in-a-Blanket with Spicy Dipping Sauce

Serves 4

DIPPING SAUCE

- 1 cup rice vinegar
- 1 teaspoon soy sauce
- 1 shallot, minced
- ½ jalapeño pepper, thinly sliced
- 1 tablespoon chopped cilantro
- 1 tablespoon orange zest
- 1 tablespoon slivered red pepper

- 4 cloves garlic, minced
- 2 tablespoons Thai fish sauce
- 1 tablespoon rice vinegar
- 1 tablespoon sesame oil
- 1 tablespoon chopped cilantro root
- 8 coriander seeds, crushed
- 12 large shrimp, peeled with tails left on
- 6 3-inch square wonton skins, halved
  Canola oil for sautéing (about ½ cup)
  Diced red peppers, chopped chives,
  and cilantro sprigs for garnish

This is an Asian update of the old cocktail party favorite, pigs-in-a-blanket. The briny dipping sauce boldly cuts through the fried wonton.

In a small bowl, combine all the ingredients for the dipping sauce and set aside.

In a shallow, nonreactive pan, combine garlic, fish sauce, rice vinegar, sesame oil, cilantro root, and coriander. Add shrimp and toss to coat. Cover and marinate, refrigerated, for ½ hour.

Remove the shrimp from marinade and pat dry. Wrap each shrimp in a wonton skin, leaving the tip and tail exposed. Brush wonton with water and press to seal.

Cover the bottom of a large sauté pan with canola oil; bring to medium heat. Sauté shrimp until pink and wontons are slightly browned, about one minute per side. Drain on paper towels.

Place a small bowl of the dipping sauce on each of 4 plates. Scatter red peppers and chives around the bowl, and arrange the shrimp, 3 per plate. Garnish with cilantro sprigs.

Asian Barbecued Pork with Mango-Pepper Relish

Serves 4

I serve this pork dish with black beans and baby bananas. The marinade works well for just about anything you grill.

PORK

- 1 tablespoon grated fresh ginger
- 1½ tablespoons soy sauce
- 1½ tablespoons sesame oil
- 1 tablespoon black-bean garlic paste
- 1 tablespoon rice vinegar
- 1 tablespoon molasses
- 2 tablespoons chopped fresh cilantro
- 2 cloves garlic, minced
- ⅛ teaspoon freshly ground black pepper
- 12 ounces pork tenderloin, trimmed of silver skin and small end tied under

RELISH

- 1 cup finely diced fresh mango
- ⅓ cup finely diced red bell pepper
- 2 tablespoons chopped crystallized ginger
- 1 tablespoon rice vinegar
- 2 tablespoons grated fresh coconut
- 1 scallion, thinly sliced
- ½ small jalapeño pepper, cored, seeded, ribs removed, minced
- 1 teaspoon grated lime zest
- 1 tablespoon chopped fresh mint

To prepare pork: In a shallow, nonreactive baking dish, combine all ingredients except pork. Add pork and turn to coat. Cover and marinate, refrigerated, for 2 hours or overnight.

Preheat oven to 450° F. Drain marinade. Remove pork and pat dry.

Return to dish and roast the pork 20-30 minutes, until the meat's internal temperature is 155° F. Let rest 10 minutes, then thinly slice.

To make relish: Combine all relish ingredients except mint. Chill, covered, until ready to use. Stir in mint before serving.

To serve: Divide black beans (recipe follows) and mound in the center of each of 4 plates. Ring each plate with the mango-pepper relish. Arrange pork slices, fanned out, around the beans. Garnish with fresh cilantro sprigs.

Black Beans & Baby Bananas

Serves 4

---

8 baby bananas, about ¾ pound,
   peeled and chopped
¼ cup lime juice
1 teaspoon canola oil
1 small red onion, chopped
2 teaspoons chili powder
1½ teaspoons ground cumin

⅛ teaspoon cayenne pepper
3 cups cooked black beans
⅓ cup chicken stock
   Salt
3 tablespoons chopped fresh cilantro
   leaves

In a small bowl, toss bananas in lime juice. Set aside.

In a large nonstick sauté pan, heat oil. Add red onion, chili powder, cumin, and cayenne pepper, and sauté until the onions are translucent, 3-4 minutes. Add black beans, chicken stock, salt to taste, and the reserved banana mixture, and heat through. Remove from heat and stir in cilantro.

Wild Asian Salad
with Ginger-Sesame Dressing

Serves 4

DRESSING
¼ cup rice wine vinegar
2 tablespoons soy sauce
1 tablespoon finely minced red sweet
   ginger, plus 1 tablespoon of its juice
   Salt & freshly ground black pepper
1 tablespoon sesame oil
1 tablespoon canola oil

SALAD
   Canola oil for sautéeing
4 3-inch-square wonton skins,
   cut in ½-inch-wide strips

¾ ounce rice stick
1 small head napa cabbage, thinly
   sliced
1 red bell pepper, slivered
¼ cup loosely packed fresh cilantro
   leaves
½ package enoki mushrooms
3 scallions, diagonally sliced
2 tablespoons toasted slivered
   almonds
   Daikon or radish sprouts for garnish

(continued on next page)

The red ginger in the dressing brings a flavorful balance of sweet and heat, and its magenta hue is a bright splash against the napa cabbage. A piece of grilled tuna, chicken, or even Asian Barbecued Pork atop this salad will transform it from side dish to a great entrée.

(Wild Asian Salad continued)

To make dressing: In a blender, combine vinegar, soy sauce, red sweet ginger and juice, and salt and pepper to taste. With the blender running, slowly drizzle in the oils. Taste and adjust the seasonings. Set aside.

To make salad: Pour ½ inch canola oil into a large sauté pan over medium-high heat. Sauté wonton strips until golden, about 1 minute. Remove the strips, drain on paper towels and set aside.

Meanwhile, add rice stick to the hot oil in small bunches. Cook until puffed up, 5-10 seconds, turning once. Drain and set aside.

In a large mixing bowl, combine cabbage, bell pepper, cilantro, mushrooms, scallions, almonds, and ½ cup of the reserved dressing. Toss gently.

Arrange salad on serving platter or divide among 4 plates. Garnish with daikon or other radish sprouts, the reserved wonton skins, and rice stick.

Polenta Pound Cake

Makes 2 loaves

Polenta pound cake is the key ingredient to my New World bread pudding.

1¼ cups all-purpose flour
1½ teaspoons baking powder
½ teaspoon salt
½ teaspoon ground star anise (optional)
¼ cup (½ stick) unsalted butter, room temperature

1 cup packed brown sugar
½ cup granulated sugar
5 large eggs
¾ cup sour cream
¾ teaspoon almond extract
½ teaspoon pure vanilla extract
1 cup cornmeal

Preheat oven to 350° F.

Grease two 1½-quart, 8½ x 4½ x 2½-inch loaf pans.

In a small mixing bowl, sift together flour, baking powder, salt, and star anise. Set aside.

In a large mixing bowl, cream butter and both sugars until creamy. Add eggs one at a time, beating after each addition.

Beat in sour cream, almond extract, and vanilla extract.

Stir in the reserved flour mixture and cornmeal.

Pour into the prepared pans and bake about 45 minutes, until a toothpick comes out clean. Cool on a wire rack for 5 minutes; remove from pans. Cool thoroughly before slicing.

Ginger-Scented Pear Pound-Pudding

Serves 12

2   cups heavy cream
3   cups milk
5   large eggs
5   egg yolks
1   cup sugar
½   teaspoon salt
1   tablespoon pure vanilla extract

¼   cup finely julienned crystallized ginger
2   loaves Polenta Pound Cake, recipe opposite
3   ripe pears (about 1½ pounds), peeled, cored, and sliced
    Freshly grated nutmeg
½   cup sliced almonds, lightly toasted

Preheat oven to 325° F. Grease an 8½ x 12½ x 2-inch nonreactive baking pan.

In a medium-sized saucepan over high heat, combine cream and milk and heat to scalding. Remove from heat and set aside.

In a large mixing bowl, whisk together eggs, egg yolks, sugar, salt, and vanilla extract. Temper the eggs by slowly adding 1 cup of the warm milk and cream. Stir in the remaining milk and cream and strain. Add ginger and let infuse for 10 minutes.

Trim the ends from the loaves of pound cake and slice into ¼-inch-thick slices. Place the slices side by side, lengthwise in the prepared pan. Tuck pears between the cake slices. Strain the ginger from the custard, reserving the custard, and tuck the ginger between the cake slices with the pears. The cake and pears should be layered vertically. Pour the custard over the pound cake and pears to cover. Sprinkle nutmeg and almonds on top.

Place pan in a larger roasting pan and fill the roasting pan with water two-thirds of the way up the pound cake pan. Bake for 1 hour and 45 minutes-2 hours, until set. Serve warm.

I thought this dessert would be great in the fall and winter as a warm comfort food, but when I took it off the menu during a hot summer month, everyone complained. I serve it on a drizzle of caramel sauce.

Teresa Rovito

A NATIVE OF MILAN, ITALY, Teresa Rovito came to the United States when she was sixteen. An interest in French literature and culture led to her work as a translator. Later, she and her husband opened a number of French restaurants in different cities, where Rovito worked in both the kitchen and the dining room. When she finally settled in New York, Rovito wanted to return to her roots — the cuisine of Italy.

Italian traditions have informed and inspired Rovito's restaurants. When she was a child, her grandmother ran a small restaurant near Milan. The drink she would serve to "the ladies who lunch" was *rosolio*, a sweet Italian liqueur flavored with rose petals. The memory of this tradition inspired the name of one of Rovito's restaurants, Rosolio, in Greenwich Village, and when it's available, she imports the rare liqueur.

Rovito's latest venture, Le Streghe, opened in 1994 and has become a popular destination in trendy Soho. "Le Streghe is my baby. I've been involved in other restaurants, but this one has all the best elements of all I've learned. It's everything I want a restaurant to be." The restaurant is open from lunch until 4 A.M. Rovito believes there should be an Italian restaurant in New York where people can eat pasta, pizza, and "little dishes" at the bar after midnight.

Her creative Italian fare couldn't be more authentic; many of Rovito's recipes have been handed down from generation to generation in her family, including the Risotto Mille E Una Notte (Rice of 1,001 Nights). This superb green risotto with peas, prosciutto, mushrooms, and spinach puree is served with a delicate prosciutto rose on the edge of bowl. Many of her dishes cannot be found elsewhere in New York, such as the delicate gnocchi with saffron cream sauce or the salmon fillet wrapped in parchment paper and baked in fresh clay. In a city full of Italian restaurants, Rovito's have always been singled out for their distinctive offerings.

For this meal, Teresa Rovito presents a selection of her favorite tastes of Italy, including a rich and elegant carpaccio, the creamy green risotto, and a savory baked chicken.

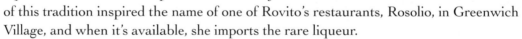

Warm Veal Carpaccio with Caper Sauce

Serves 4

2½ cups white wine
3½ tablespoons chopped scallions
2¼ cups heavy cream
1½ tablespoons chopped capers

2½ teaspoons grainy mustard
12 ounces veal fillet
Salt & freshly ground black pepper
Mesclun salad mix for garnish

Elegant but easy, this variation on the classic carpaccio makes a wonderful antipasto course.

In a saucepan, combine wine and scallions over medium heat. Reduce mixture by three-quarters. Add cream and reduce by one-quarter. Strain the sauce and set aside to cool. Add capers, mustard, and salt and pepper to taste.

Preheat oven to 500° F. Slice veal and pound thin. Arrange on a plate and place in oven for about 8 seconds. Remove from oven and pour sauce over the meat. Decorate with mesclun salad.

Bruschetta

Serves 4

1½ pounds plum tomatoes, cut into
    small chunks
2 cloves garlic, minced
10 fresh basil leaves, chopped

¼ cup extra virgin olive oil
    Salt & freshly ground black pepper
4 slices fresh country bread

In a bowl, combine tomatoes, garlic, basil, oil, and salt and pepper to taste. Blend well and marinate for one hour. Preheat the broiler. Toast the bread briefly under the broiler. Mound the tomato mixture on the toasted bread and serve.

For a simply delicious appetizer, there is no match for the flavors of fresh tomatoes, basil, and the best virgin olive oil spilling over crusty toasted bread.

Green Risotto

Serves 4

4 cups chicken stock
10 tablespoons butter
¼ cup chopped onion
1 cup Arborio rice
½ cup dry white wine
⅓ cup diced carrots
⅓ cup diced prosciutto di Parma
¼ cup diced porcini mushrooms

¼ cup green peas
⅓ cup spinach puree
2 ounces (1 cup) grated Parmesan
    cheese
    Salt & freshly ground black pepper
8 slices prosciutto di Parma rolled into
    a rose shape

In a large stockpot, bring chicken stock to a simmer over high heat. In a separate saucepan, melt 6 tablespoons of butter, add onions and sauté for 5 minutes or until pale golden. Add rice and toast for about 1 minute. Add wine and cook until evaporated. Add carrots, diced prosciutto, and mushrooms. Add ½ cup of the chicken stock. Stir constantly with a wooden spoon, loosening the rice from the sides and bottom of the pan. When the stock has evaporated, add ½ cup more stock. Keep stirring and adding stock ½ cup at a time. Continue to cook, stirring and adding broth until rice will not absorb any more liquid.

The rice is done when it's tender and cooked through, but firm to the bite, about 15 minutes longer. When the rice is done, stir in peas, spinach puree, remaining 4 tablespoons butter, and Parmesan cheese. Remove from heat and add salt and pepper to taste.

Garnish each serving dish with 2 prosciutto roses.

This recipe has been handed down for generations from my family in Italy. We call it "Risotto Mille E Una Notte," Rice of 1,001 Nights.

Chicken in Red Wine Sauce

Serves 4

A rich wine sauce complements the beautifully browned and herb-scented chicken.

4 small free-range chickens
4 bay leaves
  Olive oil for sautéing
  Salt & freshly ground black pepper
4½ cups red wine

6 tablespoons chopped scallions
2¼ cups beef stock
10 tablespoons butter, cut into small pieces

Preheat oven to 500° F.

Debone the chickens, leaving only the bone of the lower leg. Stuff 1 bay leaf into each chicken and close with 2 toothpicks. In an ovenproof skillet sauté chicken in olive oil until brown on both sides, about 10 minutes. Season with salt and pepper. Drain off excess fat. Place skillet in oven and cook for 20 minutes, or until juices run clear when leg is pierced.

In a saucepan, combine wine and scallions over high heat. Reduce by three quarters. Add stock and reduce again. Remove from heat, add butter, and strain.

When chicken is done, add sauce and serve. Remove bay leaves before eating.

iramisu

Serves 6

1½ tablespoons sugar
4 large eggs, separated
8 ounces mascarpone cheese
1 cup espresso coffee

1 tablespoon coffee liqueur
24 egg cookies or ladyfingers
Cocoa powder

In a large bowl, beat sugar and egg yolks together until pale yellow. Add mascarpone and mix for a few seconds. Do not overbeat.

In a small bowl, beat egg whites until stiff. Fold whites into mascarpone mixture.

In a small bowl, combine espresso and coffee liqueur. Dip cookies into espresso, then place one layer in an 8 x 8 deep-dish pan or trifle bowl. Cover with half the mascarpone mixture. Add another layer of dipped cookies. Top with remaining mascarpone mixture. Sprinkle with cocoa powder and refrigerate.

Tiramisu is a truly Italian dessert, with its mascarpone cheese from the Lombardy region, and its espresso-fueled flavor.

Monique Barbeau

I THOUGHT IT WOULD BE A GREAT WAY to get out of Vancouver and see another part of the world." That's how Monique Barbeau viewed her enrollment at the Culinary Institute of America in Hyde Park, New York. After graduation she found herself in the thick of the New York cooking scene. She had set a goal for herself to work at several four-star restaurants in a concentrated time period. Mission accomplished— within five years she had worked at The Quilted Giraffe, Chanterelle, and the renowned seafood restaurant Le Bernardin.

Barbeau had no professional experience when she was hired at The Quilted Giraffe. She was inspired by her time there, and the feedback and insights she received made her realize "that this is not rocket science—I can do this." She says that Gilbert Le Coze at Le Bernardin taught her a great deal about cooking fish, but she is especially appreciative of the wisdom he offered on the demands of running a kitchen, and how to attain perfection every day.

Since 1992 Barbeau has earned accolades as the executive chef at Fuller's Restaurant in Seattle. She was named Seattle's best chef in 1995, has appeared on Julia Child's television series "In Julia's Kitchen with Master Chefs," and has won a James Beard Award. Although she doesn't think the Seattle restaurant scene has the competitive edge of San Francisco or New York, Barbeau feels it will evolve as a major force in the next five years.

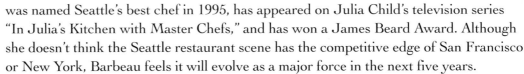

"I don't cook Northwest cuisine, whatever that is. I say my cuisine is globally influenced and regionally inspired. As I travel around the world I like to pair new ideas from new places with the ingredients I have in Seattle." About 80 percent of the menu at Fuller's is devoted to seafood. Some of Barbeau's imaginative offerings include tequila-cured gravlax on cornbread with jalapeño coulis, a tuna "taco" with cilantro pesto and cucumber sauce, sumac-dusted watermelon and cucumber salad, sweet and bitter greens with crispy fried onion and roasted beet-shallot vinaigrette, and glorious desserts that include the white caramel mousse napoleon featured here.

For this menu Monique Barbeau puts her special imprint on dishes that celebrate some of the key ingredients of the Pacific Northwest—Dungeness crab, salmon, Oregon blue cheese, and Washington apples.

*W*atercress Soup
with Finnan Haddie Brandade

Serves 10

SOUP

½ cup (1 stick) unsalted butter
5 cups chopped onions
4-5 potatoes, peeled and cut into eighths
6 cups chicken stock
2 pounds finnan haddie
2½ cups cream
6 bunches watercress
2 tablespoons fresh lemon juice
Salt & freshly ground black pepper

To make soup: In a stockpot, melt butter over medium heat. Add onions and gently sauté until soft. Add potatoes and chicken stock and bring liquid to a boil. Reduce heat to low; simmer until potatoes are soft. Meanwhile, in a large saucepan, steep finnan haddie in cream until warm. Pour into stockpot, add watercress, and stir for 30 seconds, until watercress is wilted. Immediately puree in small batches in the blender and return to pan. Season with lemon juice and salt and pepper to taste.

WATERCRESS PESTO

1 bunch watercress, stemmed and washed
1 bunch fresh Italian parsley, stemmed and washed
1 teaspoon chopped garlic
2 teaspoons chopped shallots
1½ lemons, juiced
1 cup olive oil
Salt & freshly ground black pepper

To make pesto: Place watercress, parsley, garlic, shallots, and lemon juice in a blender. Pulse to blend. Drizzle in the oil to create a smooth emulsification. Add salt and pepper to taste.

To assemble: Ladle a generous amount of warm soup into bowls and garnish with a spoonful of the pesto.

I created this soup on returning from Spain in the spring of 1995. I was inspired by Spanish cuisine's many uses for brandade (a smoked fish puree) and incorporated it here. The watercress pesto offers a subtle pepper overtone.

cs

Dungeness Crab Cakes with Asian Vinaigrette

Serves 8

VINAIGRETTE

- ½ cup fresh lime juice
- ½ cup chopped shallots
- 2 tablespoons soy sauce
- 1½ tablespoons grated fresh ginger
- ¼ cup chopped jalapeño peppers
- ½ tablespoon chopped garlic
- 2 tablespoons honey
- 1½ tablespoons curry paste
- 2 tablespoons sesame oil
- 1 cup olive oil

CRAB CAKES

- 2 tablespoons unsalted butter
- ½ red bell pepper, finely diced
- ½ yellow bell pepper, finely diced
- 1 pound Dungeness crabmeat
- 1 cup chopped daikon sprouts
- 3 tablespoons chopped fresh cilantro
- 1 cup chopped radicchio
- 1 carrot, julienned
- 1 cup panko (Japanese breadcrumbs)
- ½ cup fresh breadcrumbs
- 2 tablespoons chopped fresh ginger mixed with ½-¾ cup mayonnaise
  Salt & freshly ground black pepper
  Olive oil

To make vinaigrette: In a small bowl, whisk together all ingredients. Set aside.

To make crab cakes: In a small sauté pan, melt butter over medium heat. Add red and yellow peppers and sauté until soft, but not brown. In a large bowl combine crabmeat, sautéed peppers, daikon sprouts, cilantro, radicchio, and carrots. Add ½ cup of the panko, breadcrumbs, and enough ginger mayonnaise for ingredients to stick together. Add salt and pepper to taste.

Form crab mixture into 8 patties and lightly coat with the remaining ½ cup panko.

In a large sauté pan, heat the oil over medium heat. Once oil is hot, sauté the crab cakes until golden brown, about 3-4 minutes per side.

To serve, whisk the vinaigrette again and drizzle on each of eight plates. Place a crab cake in the center of each plate.

Oregon Blue Cheese Salad with Warm Apple Fritters

Serves 8

DRESSING

- ¼ cup chopped sweet onions
- ¼ cup red wine vinegar
- ¼ cup olive oil, plus more to coat onions
- ¼ cup salad oil
- ¼ pound blue cheese, crumbled
  Salt & freshly ground black pepper

SALAD

- 12 ounces mixed wild greens with fresh herbs (arugula, parsley, chervil), washed, dried, and torn
- ½ cup long-cut chives
- 12 cherry tomatoes cut in half
- 12 yellow cherry tomatoes cut in half
  Salt & freshly ground black pepper

FRITTERS

- 1 small Granny Smith apple, cored and finely diced
  Juice of 1 lemon,
- 4 tablespoons (½ stick) unsalted butter
- ⅔ cup all-purpose flour, plus more for breading
- 1 pound Oregon blue cheese
- 3 egg yolks
- 2 teaspoons Dijon mustard
  Salt & freshly ground black pepper
- 1 egg, mixed with water
  Breadcrumbs (ground-up croutons are best)
  Oil for frying

To make dressing: In a large sauté pan, sauté onions in enough oil to lightly coat them until they are nicely browned and tender. Let cool slightly.

Place onions in a blender with vinegar and pulse to puree. Slowly drizzle olive oil and salad oil into the running blender to emulsify. Pour the mixture into a bowl and season to taste with salt and pepper. Fold in blue cheese. Cover and refrigerate until ready to use.

To make fritters: In a small bowl, coat apples with lemon juice and set aside.

Melt butter in a large saucepan over medium heat. Stir in flour and cook slightly. Add cheese in batches until incorporated. Fold in yolks and mustard. Season with salt and pepper to taste.

Fold apples into the cheese mixture.

Spread mixture in a pan and chill for at least two hours. Form into 8 patties and chill again.

Dip each patty into flour, egg wash, and breadcrumbs. Keep cold until ready to fry.

In a deep fryer or heavy skillet, heat oil to about 350° F. Fry patties until golden brown and hot inside, about 3 minutes, making sure the oil doesn't get too hot. Blot the fritters on a paper towel.

To assemble: Place greens and chives in a large bowl and toss with the reserved dressing. Season to taste with salt and pepper. Divide the greens and pile high onto 8 plates. Arrange tomatoes artfully in and around the greens. Place one fritter on top of each salad.

The state of Oregon produces a mild, well-rounded blue cheese, and Washington is the largest apple-producing state in the nation. This salad is a tribute to the wonderful ingredients indigenous to the Northwest.

In the Pacific Northwest we are blessed with fabulous salmon, so I'm constantly trying to find innovative ways to cook it. This recipe is also great with grilled salmon. The sauce complements the taste and texture of the salmon. Serve with couscous.

∽

A delicious and light summer dessert.

∽

Sautéed Salmon with Curry-Yogurt Sauce

Serves 8

1⅓ cups yogurt	Salt & freshly ground black pepper
⅓ cup chopped shallots	8 8-ounce salmon fillets
4 teaspoons biryani (Indian curry paste)	2 teaspoons salt
	2 teaspoons pepper
4 teaspoons fresh lemon juice	4 tablespoons olive oil
4 teaspoons extra virgin olive oil	2½ tablespoons chopped mint

In a small bowl, combine yogurt, shallots, biryani, lemon juice, and olive oil. Mix well, season with salt and pepper to taste and set aside. *(The sauce may be covered and refrigerated for up to 4 days).*

In a large sauté pan, heat olive oil over medium-high heat. Sprinkle salmon on both sides with salt and pepper. Sear the salmon until golden brown, about 1 minute. Flip the fillets and finish cooking until they are browned on the outside and opaque on the inside, about 4 minutes. If the fillets are especially thick, transfer to a 400° F oven and finish cooking for 6-8 minutes.

Stir mint into the sauce. Place the salmon on a serving platter, and top with the sauce.

White Caramel Mousse Napoleon

Serves 10

PHYLLO
- 12 sheets phyllo (9 x 13-inch size)
- ½-¾ cup (1-1½ sticks) unsalted butter, melted
- ½ cup sugar

BERRY COULIS
- 4 cups fresh raspberries
- ¼ cup sugar
- ⅓ cup fresh lemon juice
- ⅓ cup fresh orange juice

CARAMEL SAUCE
- 2 cups sugar
- ⅔ cup water
- 1 cup cream

CRÈME ANGLAISE
- 2 egg yolks
- ¼ cup sugar
- 1 cup cream
- ½ vanilla bean, split and scraped

MOUSSE
- 1 pound white chocolate, rough chopped
- ½ cup crème anglaise
- 2 egg whites, room temperature
- ½ cup (1 stick) unsalted butter, room temperature
- 4 cups heavy cream, medium-whipped
- 1 cup caramel sauce

To prepare phyllo: Preheat oven to 350° F. Lightly coat a baking sheet with butter.

Carefully place one layer of phyllo on a work surface. Brush the layer with melted butter. Place another layer on top. Brush with butter and sprinkle generously with sugar. Place another layer on top and brush with butter. Place the fourth layer on top, brush with butter and sprinkle with sugar. Repeat process with remaining phyllo sheets.

Cut out 3-inch circles of the dough. Place the circles on the prepared baking sheet. Bake for 5-7 minutes or until golden brown.

To make coulis: In a blender combine 2 cups of the raspberries, sugar, lemon juice, and orange juice. Process until smooth. Pass through a strainer. Refrigerate.

To make caramel sauce: In a medium-sized saucepan, combine sugar and water over high heat. Heat to a boil. Do not stir with a spoon; instead, swirl the pan. Cook the syrup to deep golden brown. Remove from heat and slowly add cream, whisking constantly. Set aside to cool.

To make crème anglaise: In a medium-sized bowl combine yolks and sugar, whisking slightly.

In a saucepan, gently heat cream with vanilla bean over medium heat. Add about ¼ of the hot cream to the reserved egg mixture and incorporate. Pour this egg mixture back into the remaining hot cream and whisk. Continue cooking until liquid thickens. Strain. Cool in an ice bath.

To make mousse: In a double boiler over medium heat, melt white chocolate in a

stainless steel bowl. Remove from heat, whisk in crème anglaise and egg whites. Add butter and stir until melted. Fold in cream. Lightly fold in caramel sauce.

To assemble: Place a phyllo circle in the center of a plate, and place a heaping spoonful of mousse in the center. Add a few raspberries and place another layer of phyllo on top. Repeat with mousse, berries, and phyllo, finishing with a phyllo circle. Garnish plate with fresh fruit and drizzle the reserved coulis over the top.

Kathy Cary

Southern Progressive Fare

❧

Cornmeal-Avocado
Blini with
White Corn-
Poblano Salsa

———

Warm
Spinach-Portobello
Tart with
Roasted Tomato
Vinaigrette

———

Sea Scallops
with
Apple-Cider Jelly
& Creamy Leeks

———

Old-Fashioned
Oatmeal Cake
with
Orange-Basil
Ice Cream

CHARDONNAY
Grgich Hills
or
De Loach

LOUISVILLE is not generally considered to be one of America's culinary capitals, but Kathy Cary has single-handedly put her old Kentucky home on the map. Her French-inspired use of traditional Kentucky ingredients with unexpected, contemporary twists has garnered attention for her food both locally and nationally.

Growing up on a "gentleman's farm," Cary helped plant, harvest, can, and freeze some of the family's crops. As a teenager she helped in the kitchen when her mother entertained, and it was then that she discovered she was more interested in the cooking than the growing.

While working in Washington, D.C., Cary saw an ad for Cordon Bleu cooking classes and landed a job assisting the teacher. Suddenly she was introduced to a cooking style as totally different from the traditional Kentucky fare as chocolate soufflé is from chess pie. By age eighteen, she had started a catering business that was very successful with the political scene in D.C. in the early '70s—among her clients were Ted Kennedy, Henry Kissinger, and Tom Brokaw.

Cary returned to Louisville, and at age twenty was hired to manage and cook for a restaurant that prided itself on changing the menu every night. After a year of working twenty-hour days she vowed she would always own her own business. In 1979 Cary opened a gourmet take-out and catering business, La Pêche (the peach), named after "the most perfect thing you could possibly eat, in taste, texture, and smell." In 1987 she opened her restaurant, Lilly's, which draws devoted fans from around the region and has won kudos from food writers and restaurant critics across the country.

Cary takes an international approach with local ingredients. "I take the best I can get out of any growing season—April through October are really exciting months for us," Cary explains. "I'm like a kid in a toy store." She enjoys developing recipes and designing menus that offer comfort food with a new slant. "I like to go back to the basics of a dish, research it, perfect it, and add ingredients that take it to another level." She might take traditional Kentucky chicken and dumplings and transform the dish into roast chicken served on caramelized onions with gorgonzola dumplings and jalapeño plum relish. She experiments with herb ice creams as an alternative to ho-hum vanilla ice cream and fruit sherbets. The results are startlingly delicious.

Kathy Cary's food is progressive but accessible. She opts to create food that sings a familiar refrain in a simple, fresh way. Her recipes, such as Old-Fashioned Oatmeal Cake with Orange-Basil Ice Cream, invite people for a taste that recalls Mom's kitchen, yet they find something distinct and elegant enough for any occasion.

Cornmeal-Avocado Blini with White Corn-Poblano Salsa

Serves 4

SALSA

- ½ tablespoon olive oil
- 1 tablespoon chopped poblano pepper
- 1 tablespoon diced red bell pepper
- ¼ cup diced red onion
- 1½ ears sweet white corn (or ¾ cup kernels)
- ¼ lime, juiced
- ¼ teaspoon Tabasco sauce
- ¼ teaspoon salt
  Pinch of pepper
- ½ tablespoon chopped cilantro
- ¼ cup sour cream

BLINI

- 2 large eggs
- ½ cup all-purpose flour
- 2½ tablespoons cornmeal
- ½ teaspoon salt
- ¼ cup milk
- 1 ripe avocado
- ⅛ teaspoon cayenne pepper
- 2 tablespoons unsalted butter

To make salsa: In a skillet, heat oil over medium heat. Add peppers and onions, cook until wilted, 2-3 minutes. Add corn and sauté briefly. Remove from heat and toss with lime juice, Tabasco, salt, pepper, and cilantro.

To make blini: Place eggs, flour, cornmeal, salt, milk, avocado, and cayenne pepper into a blender or food processor. Blend well.

In a sauté pan or skillet, melt 1 tablespoon of butter. Add small dollops of batter to make pancakes that are half-dollar size. Turn when underside is golden; they cook quickly. Repeat with remaining butter and batter in batches. Turn onto a platter and keep warm.

To assemble: Top each warm blini with 1 teaspoon of sour cream and cover with a thin layer of salsa before serving.

This is a delicious twist on a traditional blini—a refreshing beginning to a rich but healthy meal. The salsa is straight from our Kentucky farmers with its sweet white corn, cilantro, and poblano peppers. ❧

Warm Spinach-Portobello Tart with Roasted Tomato Vinaigrette

Serves 4

CRUST

- 4 ounces cream cheese
- 1 cup (2 sticks) margarine
- 1 teaspoon salt
- 1¼ cups all-purpose flour

FILLING

- 3 pounds ripe tomatoes
- 2½ teaspoons chopped garlic
- ⅓ cup plus 3 tablespoons extra virgin olive oil
- ½ teaspoon salt
- ½ teaspoon pepper
- ⅓ cup balsamic vinegar
- ¾ pound portobello mushrooms, stemmed, cut into thin strips
- ¼ pound spinach, stemmed, washed, dried, and cut into thin strips
- ½ pound fresh mozzarella, julienned
  Capers for garnish (optional)

To make crust: Preheat oven to 375° F.

In a food processor, mix cream cheese and margarine until well combined. Add salt and flour; mix until a ball forms. Refrigerate. Roll out on a floured surface to fit an 8-inch fluted tart pan. Weight with pie weights, beans or rice in foil, and bake for 15 minutes. Cool. Remove from pan and set aside.

To make filling: Plunge tomatoes into simmering water for 15 seconds. Drain. Remove skin and seeds. Place tomatoes in roasting pan with ½ teaspoon of the garlic, ⅓ cup of the olive oil, and ¼ teaspoon each of the salt and pepper. Bake for 1½ hours. Cool slightly and coarsely chop. In a small saucepan, bring vinegar to a boil, and cook until reduced to 2 tablespoons. Add reduced vinegar to the tomato mixture and set aside.

In a large skillet, heat 2 tablespoons of the olive oil over medium heat. Add the remaining 2 teaspoons garlic and cook until golden. Remove and set aside.

In the same skillet, add the remaining tablespoon of the olive oil. Increase heat and sear portobello strips on all sides until browned. Stir in the reserved garlic and turn off the heat but keep warm.

To assemble: Place spinach in the cooled tart shell. Arrange warm portobellos like spokes of a wheel on top of spinach. Sprinkle with salt and pepper. Top with mozzarella. *(The tart may be assembled to this point and set aside.)*

Preheat the broiler. Broil briefly until cheese is melted. Drizzle each slice with tomato vinaigrette, garnish with capers and serve warm.

Held in a crisp tart shell, what you have here is really a warm salad course. The seared portobellos warm the fresh spinach, and when the whole tart is finished quickly under the broiler, the salad is ready to slice. The roasted tomato vinaigrette celebrates summer's bounty.

Sea Scallops with Apple-Cider Jelly & Creamy Leeks

Serves 4

2	cups fresh apple cider		¼	teaspoon pepper
1	large sweet potato		1	pound sea scallops, sliced in half horizontally
	Vegetable oil for frying			
1½	cups heavy cream		1	tablespoon Dijon mustard
3	cups chopped leeks		1	teaspoon fresh thyme
4	tablespoons unsalted butter		2	tablespoons olive oil
¼	teaspoon kosher salt			

In a small saucepan, bring cider to a boil over high heat. Cook quickly, stirring, until cider is reduced to ¼ cup. Set aside. It will form a jelly.

Peel sweet potato; then with the peeler, cut wide vertical slices. In a large, deep skillet, heat vegetable oil over high heat and fry potatoes until golden brown. Drain on paper towels and set aside.

In a small saucepan, bring cream to a boil over high heat. Cook rapidly, stirring without scorching until cream is reduced to 1 cup. Set aside.

In a large skillet, sauté leeks in butter over high heat, until golden brown. Add reduced cream, and ⅛ teaspoon each of the salt and pepper. Set aside and keep warm.

Toss scallops with mustard, thyme, and the remaining ⅛ teaspoon each of the salt and pepper. Heat olive oil in a large skillet over high heat; sear scallops on both sides.

To assemble: Place leek mixture in center of each of 4 dinner plates. Arrange scallop halves, overlapping around the leeks. Drizzle the top of the sea scallops with apple cider jelly. Top the leeks with sweet potato fries.

This dish is wonderful at any time, but especially on a cool evening. Finding excellent apple cider is a key to this creation, and once you do, napping the top of each scallop with your own cider jelly results in a lush, jewel-like collage. And you can't beat the creamy leeks for a sweet and savory contrast.

Old-Fashioned Oatmeal Cake

Serves 8-12

This oatmeal cake is simply the best I've eaten. The piquant ice cream, showing off orange, ginger, and basil beside the lush cake, creates a striking dessert pairing.

CAKE

- 1 cup oatmeal
- 1¼ cups boiling water
- ½ cup (1 stick) unsalted butter
- 1 cup packed brown sugar
- 1 cup sugar
- 2 large eggs
- 1 teaspoon pure vanilla extract
- 1½ cups all-purpose flour
- ½ teaspoon ground cinnamon
- ¼ teaspoon ground nutmeg
- ½ teaspoon salt
- 1 teaspoon baking soda

TOPPING

- ¾ cup (1½ sticks) unsalted butter
- 1 cup packed brown sugar
- 1 cup coconut flakes
- 1 cup chopped pecans
- 1 teaspoon pure vanilla extract

To make cake: Preheat oven to 350° F. Lightly grease and flour a 9 x 14-inch baking pan.

In a small bowl, combine oatmeal with boiling water and set aside.

In a large mixing bowl, cream butter and sugars. Add eggs and vanilla. Beat well. Slowly add flour, cinnamon, nutmeg, salt, and soda to mixture, stirring with each addition. Stir in the reserved oatmeal.

Pour into prepared baking dish. Bake 25-30 minutes or until toothpick inserted into the center of the cake comes out clean.

To make topping: Preheat the broiler. In a large mixing bowl, combine all ingredients. Blend well. Spoon and pat the topping onto cooled cake in its pan. Place the cake under the broiler and cook until the topping is bubbly and brown sugar is cooked. Cut into squares and serve warm.

Orange-Basil Ice Cream

Serves 4

1 ½ cups light cream
1 ¼ cups sugar
  1 tablespoon sliced fresh ginger
  1 cup whipping cream

½ cup frozen orange juice concentrate
2 tablespoons chopped fresh basil
   Fresh blueberries or raspberries for garnish

Place the light cream, sugar, and ginger in a saucepan over low heat. Stir until the sugar dissolves. Remove from heat. Let cool. Pour into a bowl and stir in the whipping cream and orange juice concentrate. Chill at least 2 hours. Remove the ginger slices.

Stir in basil. Process in ice cream maker according to manufacturer's instructions.

Scoop ice cream into individual serving bowls and garnish with fresh blueberries or raspberries.

Sarah Stegner

CHICAGO NATIVE Sarah Stegner has spent her entire career to date in one place—she has been a chef at The Ritz Carlton in Chicago since 1984. Stegner says there is a strong movement among chefs to spend a little time at a lot of restaurants. "I have done just the opposite. I've spent a lot of time at one place and I think it's given me a chance to really focus on my skills. I've also had the advantage of having great chefs around me."

During her first six years there she worked under the tutelage of Fernand Gutierrez, who shared his knowledge not just about food but about the restaurant industry, and Stegner particularly values her time with him. Promoted to Chef of The Dining Room in 1990, she has distinguished herself as one of America's top young chefs. She received Rising Star Chef of the Year awards from both *Esquire* magazine and the James Beard Foundation. Under Stegner's direction, The Ritz was voted one of the best hotel dining rooms in the country by *Food & Wine* magazine.

Stegner's contemporary interpretations of classical French cooking focus on seasonal products. She likes to emphasize the vegetables and eschews heavy flavor combinations. Dinner at the restaurant: sautéed duck liver with fresh warm figs and port wine sauce, yellow tomato soup with warm goat cheese, saddle of lamb stuffed with pesto with balsamic ratatouille sauce.

For this menu Stegner takes a simple approach. "I want people to be able to use the recipes. This is a meal you can actually sit down to eat and not have to run to the kitchen every ten minutes for the next course. It's a fun way for the home cook to do something special." This colorful summer meal features chilled dishes that use seasonal ingredients at the height of their flavor.

Tricolor Roasted Peppers in Lemon Vinaigrette

Serves 4

2 large lemons	2 tablespoons honey
1 large red bell pepper	1 large bunch fresh thyme
1 large orange bell pepper	2 cloves garlic, thinly sliced
1 large yellow bell pepper	Salt & freshly ground black pepper
½ cup extra virgin olive oil	12 black olives
¼ cup rice wine vinegar	

Preheat oven to 375° F. Wrap lemons in foil and bake in the oven for 40 minutes. Allow to cool slightly. Cut the lemons in half, scrape out the pulp. Remove any seeds. Set aside.

Place peppers on a broiler pan. Roast, turning the peppers periodically for about 25 minutes, until the skins are lightly charred.

Place the peppers in a bowl covered with plastic wrap. Let cool 10 minutes, then peel the skins from the peppers. Cut each pepper into four segments, remove cores and seeds. Set aside.

In a large bowl, whisk together lemon pulp, oil, vinegar, honey, garlic, and salt and pepper. Add the thyme and roasted peppers and marinate for several hours.

Arrange the peppers on a platter with olives. Pour the marinade over the peppers and serve.

A wonderful summer dish for picnics, to accompany fresh goat cheese, or served alone. The recipe calls for a large bunch of fresh thyme. To enjoy the full effect of the marinade, don't skimp on the thyme. Marinating the peppers for several hours prior to serving allows the flavors time to marry nicely.

❧

Honey-Glazed Salmon with Apple-Watercress Salad

Serves 4

SALMON

Juice of 4 limes
¼ cup honey
2 tablespoons mustard
Salt & freshly ground black pepper
4 salmon fillets (about 5 ounces each), skinned and deboned
1 bunch fresh thyme
1 cup water
½ cup white wine

SALAD

2 heads Belgian endive, washed and dried
2 Granny Smith apples
1 tablespoon grainy mustard
1 tablespoon honey
1 tablespoon rice wine vinegar
1 tablespoon olive oil
Salt & freshly ground black pepper
4 bunches watercress, washed and stemmed

To prepare salmon: In a shallow baking dish, mix together lime juice, honey, mustard, and salt and pepper. Add salmon, and marinate for 20 minutes.

Preheat oven to 400° F.

Spread thyme in the bottom of a baking pan. Place the marinated salmon on top. Add water and white wine. Cook the fish until medium rare, about 10 minutes. Remove the pan from oven. Leave the fish in the liquid until ready to serve. *(Salmon may be prepared in advance, however it is best when served slightly warm.)*

To make salad: Quarter the 2 heads of endive. Slice thin wedges of the apples, discarding the core. Mix mustard, honey, vinegar, oil, and salt and pepper together in a bowl. Add endive, watercress, and apple. Toss well.

To assemble: Divide the salad onto 4 chilled plates. Place a piece of salmon on each salad.

This easy-to-prepare salmon dish is best late in the summer, when the apple season is just beginning and the watercress is at its peak.

Chilled Tomato & Scallop Soup

Serves 4

Sea scallops add an interesting dimension to this chilled tomato soup. It's wonderfully refreshing on a hot summer day.

5 tablespoons olive oil
1 onion, minced
8 ripe tomatoes, skinned, seeded, and chopped
   Salt & freshly ground black pepper
1 pound sea scallops

1 cup peeled and diced cucumber
1 red pepper, cored and diced
1 tablespoon chopped cilantro
1 tablespoon chopped basil
1 tablespoon chopped chives

In a medium skillet, heat 3 tablespoons olive oil. Add onions and sauté until translucent. Add tomatoes and sauté for an additional minute. Reduce heat, season with salt and pepper to taste, and simmer for about 5 minutes. Set aside to cool.

In a skillet, heat the remaining 2 tablespoons olive oil over high heat. Sear scallops until golden brown on both sides, but still tender and translucent.

Add cucumbers, red pepper, herbs, and scallops to tomato mixture. Chill before serving.

Blueberry Custard in Phyllo

Serves 4

1½ cups cream
4   large eggs
1   vanilla bean, split and scraped
¾   cup sugar
1   cup blueberries, washed and
    stemmed

8   sheets phyllo dough
    (9 x 13-inch size)
3   tablespoons melted butter
2   tablespoons sugar

Preheat oven to 325° F. Butter the bottom of an 8-inch square nonstick baking dish.

In a bowl, whisk the cream and eggs together. Add vanilla bean to the custard mixture. Whisk in sugar.

Spread the berries on the bottom of the pan and pour the custard over them. Cover with a buttered piece of parchment paper or wax paper. Bake for 45 minutes or until the custard is firm. Allow to cool, about 30 minutes. Cut the custard into 8 triangles.

Spread one sheet of phyllo dough on a cutting board, keeping the other sheets covered with a cloth so the dough will not dry out. Brush the sheet of phyllo with melted butter and sprinkle with sugar. Place another sheet on top and repeat process until you have a stack of 4 buttered sheets. Cut the phyllo into 4 equal strips. Place a custard triangle at the bottom corner of each strip and fold the triangle into the dough. Repeat the layering process again with the 4 remaining sheets of phyllo, cut into 4 strips and fold remaining 4 triangles.

Bake on a hot baking sheet for about 20 minutes until golden brown.

I like to make this dessert in August, when the best blueberries are available. You can find phyllo dough in the frozen food section of your grocery store.

$\mathcal{D}$eborah Hughes

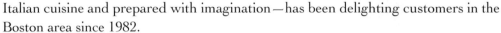

I WANT TO MAKE FOOD that speaks for itself without saying 'Look at me, here's my party hat.' I like simple food brought to its ultimate essence, with the flavors extracted so that you can experience 'the real red pepper.' I want food to become a new language on your plate." Chef Deborah Hughes is wonderfully fluent in that language. As co-owner of the Cambridge, Massachusetts, restaurant Upstairs at the Pudding, her sumptuous food—informed by northern Italian cuisine and prepared with imagination—has been delighting customers in the Boston area since 1982.

Hughes' first job in a restaurant was as a dishwasher, and she was immediately drawn to the familial aspects of the work. The restaurant was the Peasant Stock, a Cambridge favorite in the '70s, and Hughes credits her philosophy on food and business to her years there. "It was really civilized. It was the first place I had ever worked where everyone was respected and therefore treated equally. We were all paid $25, no matter what we did." Eventually it became evident that Hughes' talents were better suited to cooking than to dishwashing and she became a chef at the restaurant. Employees and customers were an eclectic bunch and included working-class locals as well as the Harvard gentry. Hughes' current business partner Mary-Catherine Deibel, a divinity student at the time, also worked at the Peasant Stock, and the two decided to open a restaurant.

To the uninitiated the name of Hughes' restaurant may be puzzling. Located across the street from historic Harvard Yard, Upstairs at the Pudding was originally the dining room of Harvard's Hasty Pudding Club, founded in 1795 as a secret society. A private dining room at the restaurant sports three crocodiles shot by club member President Teddy Roosevelt and now mounted over the fireplace.

Hughes has traveled to Italy to study the art of Italian cooking with Marcella Hazan. She continues to draw on Italian cuisine to create her richly textured yet understated dishes. She is known for her flavorful soups, like the gazpacho included in this menu as well as a spicy roasted red pepper soup and hearty Tuscan white bean soup.

Hughes notes that as cooking has become more professionalized there are many more graduates of cooking schools in the job market. But she finds that the schools don't seem to be teaching much about "the relationship between common sense, chemistry, and the work ethic, and may be robbing young chefs of their intuition. You can't be a good cook without intuition—you must learn the fundamental components and techniques, but it takes your instincts to create."

This menu features the robust seasonal flavors that are Hughes' signature.

Innovative Northern Italian

ෆ

Gazpacho
with
Pesto &
Rock Shrimp

Duck Salad
with
Roquefort Flan

Grilled Steak
Florentine
with
Tuscan White Beans

Charlotte au Chocolat

SYRAH
Swanson
or
Edmunds St. John

Gazpacho with Pesto & Rock Shrimp

Serves 4-6

2	bunches basil, washed and stemmed	2	red bell peppers, seeded and finely diced
2	cloves garlic, minced	2	yellow bell peppers, seeded and finely diced
1	teaspoon salt		
2	teaspoons sugar	1½	green bell peppers, seeded and finely diced
¼	cup balsamic vinegar		
½	cup extra virgin olive oil	1½	bunches scallions, finely diced
16	plum tomatoes, seeded and diced	⅔	red onion, finely diced
1	pound cooked rock shrimp	½	bunch fresh chives, finely diced
1½	English cucumbers		Lemon zest for garnish

In blender or food processor combine basil, garlic, salt, sugar, vinegar, and olive oil. Add pesto to tomatoes and leave at room temperature for several hours.

Split shrimp lengthwise, toss with a bit of olive oil and garlic and set aside.

Score cucumbers with a fork, seed, and finely dice. Add cucumbers, peppers, scallions, onions, and chives to tomato mixture and stir to blend flavors.

Just before serving add rock shrimp and other ingredients as desired. Garnish with lemon zest.

This versatile soup can have any number of ingredients added just before serving: sliced avocado, grilled corn or eggplant, or tiny zucchini. I especially like the rock shrimp used in this recipe. This gazpacho can be made several days in advance, and is served at room temperature instead of the more traditional chilled variety.

Duck Salad with Roquefort Flan

Serves 4

Creamy flan, tasty pieces of duck, and a savory pancetta vinaigrette provide a marvelous combination of flavors for this salad.

FLAN

- 4 ounces cream cheese
- 4 ounces sour cream
- 4 ounces Roquefort or blue cheese
- 3 egg yolks plus 1 large egg
- 1 tablespoon fresh thyme
  Salt & freshly ground black pepper
- 4 tablespoons breadcrumbs or Parmesan cheese

DUCK

- 1 whole duck
- 2 small onions
- 2 carrots
- 2 ribs celery
  Orange juice (optional)

SALAD

- 1 cup diced pancetta or cob-smoked bacon
- ½ cup plus 1 tablespoon extra virgin olive oil
- 2 tablespoons raspberry vinegar
- 2 tablespoons honey, heated
  Salt & freshly ground black pepper
- 4 cups mixed greens (radicchio, frisée, endive), washed, dried, and torn
- ½ cup diced red onion
- ½ cup olives
- 4 clementines, peeled, membrane removed

To make flan: Preheat oven to 300° F. In a food processor, blend cream cheese, sour cream, Roquefort, eggs, and thyme until smooth. Add salt and pepper to taste.

Butter the inside of four 6-8 ounce ramekins and coat lightly with bread-crumbs or Parmesan cheese. Fill the ramekins three-quarters full with the cheese mixture.

Place ramekins in a deep roasting pan and fill pan with hot water until ramekins are half-covered. Bake for 1½-2 hours, or until a knife inserted in the center comes out clean. Cool flan to room temperature before storing. *(May be made ahead and refrigerated until ready to use. Reheat in microwave for 1 minute or warm in oven just prior to serving.)*

To prepare duck: Preheat oven to 350° F. Roast duck on a bed of vegetables (onions, carrot, celery) for 2 hours. Prick with fork. Baste with orange juice.

Remove skin and break meat into 2-inch strips with hands.

To make dressing: Sauté pancetta in ½ cup olive oil until still translucent; do not overcook. Drain on paper towels. Pour oil from frying pan into bowl and whisk together with vinegar, the remaining 1 tablespoon olive oil, and honey. Add salt and pepper to taste. Drizzle duck pieces with a small amount of vinaigrette 5-10 minutes before serving. Add pancetta to vinaigrette.

To assemble: Arrange greens on 4 individual salad plates. Dress lightly with vinaigrette. Fan the duck pieces in a circle on the greens. Run a knife around the inside edge of each flan ramekin and place upside down in the center of the greens. The flan should easily fall out onto the salad. Garnish with onions, olives, and clementines.

Grilled Steak Florentine with Tuscan White Beans

Serves 4

BEANS

  1 pound large white beans
  2 sprigs rosemary or other herb
  2 ham hocks
  2 tablespoons salt
  1 cup plus 2 tablespoons olive oil
  2 heads garlic, chopped
  ½ cup lemon juice
     Salt & freshly ground black pepper

STEAKS

  6 cloves garlic
  1 cup extra virgin olive oil
  ½ cup lemon juice
  2 teaspoons kosher salt
  1 teaspoon freshly ground black pepper
  1 lemon, cut in half
  4 12-16 ounce Porterhouse steaks

To make beans: In a heavy-bottomed casserole, cover beans with water. Add herbs, ham hocks, salt, and 2 tablespoons olive oil. Cook gently over low heat for 2 hours.

Remove from heat, drain, and while still warm, add the remaining 1 cup olive oil, garlic, lemon juice, and salt and

(continued on next page)

Steak Florentine does not refer to a spinach preparation, as many of our customers have presumed. It derives its name from a special kind of steak from cows that graze outside the city of Florence. This is a wonderful high-summer dish, and can also be served with grilled tomato slices or baked garlic, but these Tuscan beans are my favorite accompaniment.

(Grilled Steak Florentine continued)

pepper to taste. Beans absorb lots of tastes before they give off flavor, so use a heavy hand in seasoning. Store at room temperature.

To prepare steaks: Marinate garlic in olive oil, lemon juice, salt, and pepper. Prick holes in each steak to tenderize. Rub half a lemon, cut side down, onto steak. Pour the marinade over the steaks, and marinate at least 3 hours or overnight.

Prepare a grill or preheat broiler.

Remove steaks from marinade and pat dry with kitchen towel. Pat steaks gently with olive oil and score fat on each steak.

Grill over hot coals or broil on a hot, seasoned cast-iron pan. Grill until rare, approximately 3 minutes on the first side and 2 minutes on the second. Remember that marinade already slightly cooks a steak.

Remove from heat, rub with salt, pepper, garlic, cut lemon, and olive oil. (Do not use marinade.) Let rest a moment to hold the juices. Slice on the diagonal in thin strips and serve on a large platter with Tuscan beans.

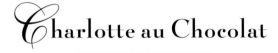

Charlotte au Chocolat

Serves 8

This is our house dessert that we have been serving since we opened. It continues to rank among our most popular sweets. For the best results, be sure to use a good quality chocolate.

8 ounces semisweet chocolate
1 cup sugar
½ cup brewed coffee, hot
½ pound (1 stick) sweet butter, softened
4 large eggs, beaten

2 tablespoons liqueur of your choice (optional)
1 cup whipping cream
   Candied violets for garnish

Preheat oven to 350° F.

In a saucepan, combine sugar and coffee and bring to a boil. Remove from heat and stir in chocolate and butter. Fold eggs into chocolate mixture and mix well. Add liqueur if desired and mix again.

Place double-folded heavy-duty aluminum foil in an 8-10 cup charlotte

mold or soufflé pan. Pour in batter. Place mold or pan in a hot water bath and bake for 45-50 minutes, or until top is firmly set. Chill. Whip the cream. Divide cake into 8 equal servings and cover with piped whipped cream. Add candied violets to garnish.

Debra Ponzek

CHARDONNAY
Kistler
or
PINOT BLANC
Chalone

AFTER TWO YEARS of engineering school, Debra Ponzek realized that it was not a field she could get passionate about, so she switched gears and headed for the Culinary Institute of America. Following her graduation in 1984 she cooked at several top restaurants in her native New Jersey.

In 1986 Drew Nieporent hired Ponzek as sous-chef at the fledgling Montrachet in New York. Only ten months later, she was promoted to chef. Her Provençal-inspired cuisine soon drew accolades, including the prestigious Rising Star Chef of the Year award from the James Beard Foundation. At the age of twenty-eight she was named as one of *Food & Wine* magazine's "Ten Best New American Chefs."

She left Montrachet in 1994 to write her first cookbook and to open a gourmet food shop, Aux Délices, in Greenwich, Connecticut. Many of her colleagues in culinary circles were surprised at her departure. Ponzek says she got the feeling that "a lot of people think that if you're not cooking at a restaurant in New York, anything else you do isn't really worthwhile. But at this point in my life I wanted to try a different aspect of the restaurant business while I was still young enough to put the time and energy into it."

Ponzek says her food combines French tradition with an American perspective. Her training in classic French cooking at the C.I.A. is the foundation for all her dishes, "but I have my own approach. I like to keep things simple, never fussy. There is a Mediterranean touch to my cooking as well. Whatever I prepare, I start with a bouquet of fresh herbs and vegetables. They inspire my colorful, aromatic combinations."

This menu exemplifies the Ponzek principle of simple elegance. "I love to cook fish and sauces. I don't do a lot of heavy brown sauces anymore, but I do a lot with herbs

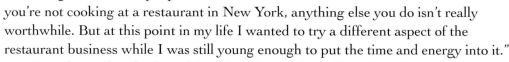

and oils like the ginger vinaigrette in this meal." Her sesame-crusted cod brings a number of simple elements together to make a sophisticated dish. The sesame seeds lend an interesting look and crunchy texture, and also serve to seal in the juices of the fish. The vinaigrette picks up the accent of the sesame seeds, and purple potatoes make for a lovely presentation. The dessert, a country-French clafouti, is a magical combination of fresh peaches topped with custard batter that is baked to creamy perfection.

Silky Corn Soup

Serves 8

12 ears sweet corn, kernels removed
(4 cups)
2 tablespoons unsalted butter
6 cups chicken stock, plus extra as
needed

1 sprig fresh tarragon
1 cup heavy cream
Salt
Pinch of cayenne pepper
Chopped chives

Place ¼ cup of the corn in a small sauce-pan over high heat, cover with cold water and bring to a boil. Drain and run under cold water. Set aside.

In a large stockpot, melt butter over medium heat. Add the remaining corn and sauté for 1 minute. Add stock and tarragon; raise the heat and bring to a boil. Reduce heat to low and simmer 20 minutes. The corn should still be covered by about an inch of stock. If there is more, keep simmering and if there is less, add a little stock. Add cream and simmer 10 more minutes.

Pour the soup into a blender in batches, and blend each batch very well. Strain through a coarse strainer. Season with salt and cayenne pepper to taste. Garnish with the reserved corn kernels and chopped chives.

This is one of my favorite soups: simple, elegant, and just a touch spicy. To really dress it up, garnish with fresh lobster or shrimp.

෫

Shrimp Salad
with White Beans & Fresh Thyme

Serves 8 as an appetizer

Pink shrimp, white beans, and bright salad greens make a beautiful dish. The classic combination of white beans and thyme marries perfectly with the sweetness of the shrimp.

ꞔꞔ

VINAIGRETTE

⅓ teaspoon salt, plus extra if needed
  Freshly ground black pepper
2 tablespoons plus 2 teaspoons finely chopped shallots
1½ sprigs fresh thyme
⅓ cup sherry vinegar, plus extra if needed
1⅓ cups extra virgin olive oil

SALAD

2 cups great Northern beans
12 sprigs fresh thyme, leaves only, roughly chopped
3 ripe tomatoes, peeled, seeded, and cut into small dice
¾ red onion, cut into small dice
4 cups mixed greens washed, dried, and torn
24 cooked jumbo shrimp, shelled
  Salt & freshly ground black pepper

To make vinaigrette: In a small bowl or jar, whisk together salt, pepper, shallots, thyme, and vinegar until the salt is dissolved. Slowly whisk in the oil until emulsified. Taste and season if necessary. Add more vinegar or oil, if needed.

To make salad: In a large saucepan, cover beans with cold water and bring to a boil. Reduce heat and simmer until tender, about 45 minutes. Drain well.

In a large mixing bowl, combine the beans with ½ cup of the vinaigrette, thyme, tomatoes, and onions. Cool to room temperature. Season to taste with salt and pepper. Makes about 4 cups beans. Set aside to cool.

When the beans have cooled, toss greens in a large bowl with ½ cup vinaigrette until lightly coated.

To assemble: For each serving, place about ½ cup of the white-bean salad on a plate and arrange the greens in 3 small mounds around them. Arrange 3 shrimp around the beans, alternating with the greens, and drizzle with the remaining vinaigrette.

Sesame-Crusted Cod
with Ginger Vinaigrette & Sautéed Potatoes

Serves 8

VINAIGRETTE

½ teaspoon salt, plus extra if needed
½ cup champagne vinegar, plus extra if needed
1 teaspoon freshly ground black pepper
1 cup plus 2 tablespoons olive oil
6 tablespoons sesame oil
2 tablespoons finely diced shallots
2 tablespoons grated fresh ginger

POTATOES

12 small purple potatoes
12 small fingerling or creamer potatoes
2 tablespoons sesame oil
2 bunches scallions, roots removed, cut 1-inch thick on the bias
 Salt & freshly ground pepper

COD

¾ cup sesame seeds, black and white mixed
8 cod steaks (6-8 ounces each)
2 teaspoons vegetable oil
 Salt & freshly ground pepper

To make vinaigrette: One day before serving, whisk together salt, vinegar, and pepper until the salt is dissolved. Slowly whisk in olive and sesame oils until emulsified. Whisk in shallots and ginger. Season to taste, if necessary. Add more vinegar if needed and refrigerate. Before using, strain through a fine strainer.

To make potatoes: In a large saucepan, cover potatoes in salted water. Bring to a boil over high heat, then reduce heat to simmer until tender, about 15 minutes. Drain and cool in the refrigerator about ½ hour.

When cool, cut potatoes in half and then into ⅛-inch slices.

In a medium nonstick pan, heat sesame oil over medium-high heat, until shimmering. Add scallions and the reserved potatoes and sauté until the

(continued on next page)

Cod crusted with a mixture of sesame seeds gives a beautiful appearance. The cod sits on a bed of colorful sautéed potatoes and scallions dressed in a fragrant ginger vinaigrette.

(Sesame-Crusted Cod continued)

scallions are tender and potatoes are light golden brown, about 10 minutes. Season with salt and pepper to taste and reserve, keeping warm.

To prepare: Place sesame seeds in a shallow bowl. Coat the fish on both sides with the sesame seeds and season with salt and pepper to taste.

In a large skillet, heat oil over high heat until just smoking and sear the cod on one side for 3 minutes. Turn and sear until fairly firm to the touch, about 5 more minutes.

Divide the potato mixture among 8 warm plates, place a piece of fish on top of each portion, and drizzle with the reserved vinaigrette.

$\mathcal{P}$each Clafouti

Serves 8

Clafouti is the simplest of desserts, classically made with cherries, but equally delicious with fresh peaches. For a more elegant presentation, bake in individual servings, or pour into a tart shell.

∞

1 tablespoon unsalted butter	6 tablespoons sifted all-purpose flour
½ cup plus 1 tablespoon sugar	1½ cups heavy cream
3 cups peeled, sliced peaches	1 tablespoon cinnamon
3 large eggs	1 tablespoon any fruit brandy
1 vanilla bean or 2 teaspoons pure vanilla extract	(optional)

Preheat oven to 375° F.

Lightly grease a 10-inch-round glass baking dish with butter and sprinkle with 1 tablespoon of the sugar. Arrange peaches on the bottom of the dish.

In a medium-sized bowl, beat eggs until fluffy. Slit vanilla bean lengthwise and scrape the seeds into the beaten eggs.

Add the remaining ½ cup of sugar, flour, cream, cinnamon, and brandy, if using. Whisk together well. Let rest at room temperature for 10 minutes.

Pour the batter over the peaches and bake about 40 minutes, until the custard is firm. Serve warm or at room temperature.

Catherine Brandel

ALTHOUGH SHE WAS TRAINED as an anthropologist at U. C. Berkeley, Catherine Brandel's love of cooking eventually overcame her scientific bent. While taking a cooking class in the late '60s she met Michael James, who, years later, asked her to help with the launch of the Great Chefs of France Cooking School at the Robert Mondavi Winery in the Napa Valley. She says, "We didn't know very much but we were *extremely* hard working and good natured—and here we were helping famous French chefs like Jean Troisgros." In the course of working at the cooking school Brandel met Alice Waters, who asked Brandel to come work at Chez Panisse. "I was terrified at the idea but was so flattered that I said yes." Brandel became the original "forager" for the legendary Berkeley, California, restaurant. This could mean anything from searching out specialty growers and purveyors to going out and picking wild mustard. She later became chef of the cafe and then, executive chef of the downstairs restaurant.

Brandel's current position as Chef-Instructor at the Culinary Institute of America's new Greystone campus in the Napa Valley seems tailor-made. As a standard-bearer for promoting sustainable agriculture and seasonal produce, Brandel is uniquely qualified to teach about the critical relationship between the quality of ingredients and how to skillfully transform them into special meals.

Brandel describes her cooking as "probably conservatively Mediterranean. The ingredients that present themselves in California are so similar. I do pretty simple food, although sometimes I look at a recipe and say—'what an elaborate recipe for such a simple dish'—but I still think of it as simple food."

She has several tales to tell of the trials of the woman chef, from her early experiences in France when she would be allowed to run the kitchen, but any task that involved approaching the stove would be given to the lowliest male rather than to a woman. "Their thinking was just so ingrained they didn't really consider what they were doing." Even recently, she tells of how, while representing Chez Panisse at benefits, she would take a male prep cook with her, and invariably, when they checked into the hotel the man would get the room with the flowers and champagne—the assumption being that he was the senior chef! Brandel believes it's important to treat these incidents with good humor. "There's no sense in getting strident. You make inroads, you show by example."

In this fall harvest menu, Brandel finds all the flavor and texture contrasts absolutely satisfying. She likes to serve this meal with a selection of cheeses, crisp Asian pears, succulent Fuyu persimmons, and newly harvested walnuts.

Shaved Vegetable Salad

Serves 6

6-8 tablespoons extra virgin olive oil

1-3 tablespoons fresh lemon juice

1 clove garlic, crushed
Salt

3 large fennel bulbs

6 celery stalks, thinly sliced on the diagonal

8 large radishes, thinly sliced

1 large bunch Italian parsley, washed, dried, leaves removed

12 anchovy fillets, preferably cleaned, salt-packed

2-3 ounce piece of Parmesan cheese, shaved with a vegetable peeler
Freshly ground black pepper

In a small bowl or jar, whisk together olive oil, lemon juice, garlic, and salt to taste. Set aside.

Trim the feathery stalks and root of fennel so the base of the bulb is flat. Remove any tough outer stalks. Using a sharp knife or mandoline, slice the bulb in half from top to bottom. Then slice crosswise as thinly as possible into half moons. In a plastic bag, toss the sliced fennel with a few drops of lemon juice to prevent discoloration. Set aside.

Just before serving, in a large bowl, toss the fennel, celery, and radishes with a little of the olive oil.

Arrange the vegetables and anchovies on 6 plates. Sprinkle with salt to taste and drizzle with the reserved lemon dressing.

Sprinkle on a generous amount of shaved Parmesan. Finish with pepper to taste.

This is a variation on an antipasto served in the Piedmont region of Italy. The success of this simple and refreshing first course depends upon all ingredients being impeccably fresh and sliced as thinly as possible.

ↄ

Grilled Pigeon Salad
with Savory Liver Toasts & Pickled Grapes

Serves 6

I chose to make a pigeon salad on my last night as Chef at Chez Panisse — it is probably my all-time favorite dish. The accompaniments to this warm salad of slightly bitter greens are mild, sweet pickled grapes, and a grilled crouton spread with buttery liver paste. You may substitute game hens or quail for the pigeon.

෬

PICKLED GRAPES

- 4 cups sugar
- 2¾ cups white wine vinegar
- 1 cup water
  Flavoring of choice, such as cinnamon sticks, allspice, bay leaves, peppercorns, or thyme, tied in a cheesecloth bag
- ½ teaspoon salt
- 2-2½ pounds seedless grapes, such as Red Flame or Thompson, washed, and stemmed

PIGEON SALAD

- 4 tablespoons extra virgin olive oil
- 4 sprigs fresh thyme
- 1 bay leaf
- 1 tablespoon sweet wine, such as Beaumes de Venise or Riesling
- 6 pigeons, boned, livers and hearts trimmed and skewered for grilling
  Salt & freshly ground black pepper
- 1 large shallot, finely minced
- 1 scant tablespoon dense balsamic vinegar
- ½ teaspoon sherry vinegar
- 1 tablespoon unsalted butter
- 8 cups mixed sturdy lettuces such as frisée, radicchio, escarole, and rocket, washed, dried, and torn
- 12 2 x 3½-inch crustless bread croutons, coated with olive oil

To make grapes: In a large saucepan over medium heat, simmer sugar, vinegar, water, seasoning bag, and salt for 5 minutes. Pour the brine over the grapes. Let cool, then refrigerate. (*The grapes will keep indefinitely in the refrigerator.*)

To make salad: In a nonreactive baking dish, stir together 2 tablespoons of the olive oil, thyme, bay leaf, and wine.

Season the pigeon breasts, legs, and hearts with salt and pepper to taste. Place in the marinade. Cover, refrigerate and marinate.

In a bowl, macerate shallots in the vinegars with a little salt for at least ½ hour. Add remaining 2 tablespoons olive oil, whisk together, and set aside.

Prepare a grill.

Season the reserved, skewered livers and grill them rare. Remove from skewer. Mash with butter and salt and pepper to taste. Set aside.

Remove the meat from the marinade. Grill the skewered hearts, breasts, and legs over a medium-hot fire, being sure to get the skin side well-caramelized. Cook until medium rare, about 4-6 minutes per side. Be sure the skin is well-browned. Keep warm, being sure to save all the juices that accumulate.

Grill the croutons until brown on both sides.

Drain and cut ½ cup of the reserved grapes. In a large metal bowl over low heat, warm the grapes with a little of the shallot dressing. Add lettuces, the rest of the dressing, and a drizzle of the grilling juices. Toss, just to take the chill off the

lettuces, but not wilt them. Check the seasoning carefully.

To assemble: Distribute the salad and the grapes on 6 plates. Add a few drops of the reserved grilling juices to the liver paste, spread on the warm croutons and top with the sliced breast meat. Nestle two croutons, the legs, and a grilled heart in the greens on the plate so as not to flatten them. Drizzle with a little more dressing and the reserved juices.

Ricotta Gnocchi
with Roasted Wild Mushrooms

Serves 6-8

Kelsie Kerr, a cook at the Zuni Cafe in San Francisco, taught me how to make these ethereally light and delicate gnocchi. Roasting enhances the flavor of a less-than-exceptional mushroom and captures every bit of the perfume of the just-collected prize.

✌

MUSHROOMS

1½ pounds wild mushrooms, such as cepes, morels, or chanterelles
    Salt & freshly ground black pepper
 2 tablespoons olive oil
½ cup white wine
 2 sprigs fresh thyme (or herbs of your choice)
2-4 tablespoons juice from roasted chicken or game bird (optional)

GNOCCHI

½ pound ricotta cheese, drained
 2 large eggs
    Scant pinch freshly ground nutmeg
1-2 ounces grated Parmesan cheese
    Salt & freshly ground black pepper
 1 tablespoon melted unsalted butter
1-3 tablespoons all-purpose flour

To make mushrooms: Preheat oven to 375° F.

If mushrooms are dry and not gritty, brush or wipe them clean. If they are very wet, hard to brush, or gritty, fill a deep bowl with water, plunge the mushrooms into the water and agitate them with your hands. Lift the mushrooms out of the water and drain. Repeat the process with clean water until the mushrooms are clean. (You should never have to do this with cepes.)

Cut mushrooms into half-inch wedges or chunks. Place in a baking pan, season with salt and pepper to taste, sprinkle with olive oil, wine, thyme sprigs or other herbs, and bird juices, if using. Cover and roast 30-40 minutes.

When a good deal of juice has rendered, pour the juice into a small saucepan and cook over medium heat until reduced by one-third. Set aside.

Increase the heat to 425° F. Uncover and brown the mushrooms slightly. Pour a little of the reduced and well-seasoned mushroom juice over the cooked mushrooms and set aside.

To make gnocchi: In a medium-sized bowl, stir ricotta with a wooden spoon until the cheese reaches a uniform consistency. Add eggs, nutmeg, Parmesan, salt and pepper to taste, and stir vigorously. Add butter, then flour in two batches. Stir in gently—gnocchi will toughen if stirred too much. *(The dough will keep, refrigerated, for 2-3 days.)*

On a floured work surface, roll dough into a cylinder shape. Cut into approximately 32 pieces and roll each piece into an oval dumpling shape with thumb.

To form and store the formed gnocchi for up to a couple of hours before serving, you can lay them out on sheet pans covered with floured parchment paper. Group a serving amount together. When ready to poach, cut off a section of the paper that has the number of gnocchi you want to serve, hold it over the pot of simmering water and scoot them into the water.

To serve: In a large pot of just-boiling salted water, simmer gnocchi gently until set in the center, not runny, about 3-4 minutes depending on the size. Remove the gnocchi from the water with a slotted spoon and gently place in shallow soup plates. Spoon roasted mushrooms into soup plates and drizzle with the reduced mushroom juices.

Cabernet-Poached Pears

Serves 6

½   bottle full-bodied red wine
1½ cups water
½-¾ cup sugar

1   sprig fresh basil or thyme
2   pounds firm ripe pears, such as Bartlett or Bosc

In a large nonreactive saucepan, combine wine, water, sugar, and basil or thyme. Bring to a simmer.

Meanwhile, leaving the stems intact, peel pears with a vegetable peeler and core them. Place pears in simmering syrup as you finish peeling them. Simmer until pears are cooked through but not mushy, 20-30 minutes.

Remove pears from syrup with a slotted spoon and reduce syrup to about three-quarters of its original volume. Let pears and syrup cool separately to room temperature, then combine and refrigerate until ready to serve.

If you are lucky enough to find the small Seckel pears in your market, they make a particularly attractive presentation for this dessert. Serve with a bowl of crème fraîche or crème anglaise on the side and your favorite cookie.

❧

Susan Spicer

IN A FAMILY with seven children, a lot of time is devoted to preparing meals, and as the sixth child, Susan Spicer spent many hours sitting on the kitchen counter watching what mom was doing. Having been born in Denmark, and having lived around the world with her Navy husband, Mom was making some pretty interesting food. Mealtime at the Spicers' might include Scandinavian food or Indonesian dishes from when the family lived in Holland. "My mother always cooked lots of different kinds of food and always enjoyed it, so cooking seemed like a pleasurable sort of thing to me," Spicer says.

Spicer didn't tap into this international heritage until the early '80s. She was corralled by a friend to work with her in a restaurant. "I was working in the printing business, in graphic arts, and it wasn't coming naturally to me. When I started working in a restaurant everything seemed to gel," Spicer recalls.

She took cooking classes, apprenticed at several restaurants, and traveled extensively to expand her culinary horizons. By 1986 she was executive chef at The Bistro at Maison de Ville in New Orleans, where she drew a loyal following. Soon she was hearing the refrain that she needed a bigger place, so in 1990 she opened Bayona in the French Quarter. There she serves a multicultural menu to admiring crowds.

Spicer's ingenuity in pairing diverse ingredients for exciting new tastes places her on the cutting edge of American cuisine. In this colorful, Asian-inspired menu, she looks to Indonesian curry and chili pastes (sambals) to play an important flavor role in several dishes. The basil-cilantro sauce in the main dish is an adaptation of a recipe she learned from a Vietnamese woman who worked for her. Usually served with duck breast or a stuffed chicken wing, here this creamy piquant sauce steps up to accent some of New Orleans' finest shrimp.

Rather than focusing on the regional Cajun and Creole food of Louisiana, Spicer takes a different approach. "To tell you the truth, I don't intellectualize it at all," she confesses. "I just cook food that I like, and try to cook food that I imagine my customers will like." The day's menu usually comes together after a trip to the walk-in refrigerator. "I look at the fruits and vegetables to see what I have and decide what the treatment is going to be. Then I might decide, our fish today is wahoo — am I going to grill or sear it? I often make a list of proteins on one side of a page and different fruits and vegetables on the other, match one from Column A with one from Column B, and take off from there."

Couscous Soup

Serves 4-6

2 tablespoons olive oil	½ teaspoon paprika
1 medium onion, chopped	¾ cup couscous
½ bunch celery, chopped	½ teaspoon sambal oelek (Indonesian chili paste)
1 carrot, chopped	
1 medium turnip, diced	Salt & freshly ground black pepper
1 red bell pepper, diced	1 teaspoon finely diced zucchini
2 fresh tomatoes, chopped (or 1-2 cups canned tomatoes)	1 teaspoon finely diced red bell pepper
1 quart chicken or vegetable broth	1 teaspoon finely diced scallions
Bouquet garni of parsley and cilantro stems, cinnamon stick and bay leaf (tied together)	1 teaspoon finely chopped cilantro leaves
	Extra virgin olive oil
1 teaspoon ground cumin	Fresh lemon juice to taste

This soup-of-many-colors looks like a bowl of edible confetti.

In a large stockpot, heat oil over high heat. Add onions, celery, carrots, turnips, and peppers and sauté until wilted, 10-15 minutes. Add tomatoes, broth, bouquet garni, cumin, and paprika and bring to a boil. Reduce heat and simmer until vegetables are tender, about 30 more minutes. Stir in ½ cup of the couscous and cook until couscous is soft, about 10 minutes.

Remove from heat, cool a bit, then remove bouquet garni. In a blender or food processor, blend soup in batches.

Strain and reheat over low heat. Season with salt, pepper, and sambal oelek and keep warm.

In a small bowl, cover the remaining ¼ cup of the couscous with ¼ cup of hot water (or broth from the soup). Let stand until tender. Stir in zucchini, red pepper, scallions, cilantro, olive oil, lemon juice, and salt.

Serve soup hot with couscous garnish.

Velvet Shrimp with Spicy Basil Sauce

Serves 4

SAUCE

¼ cup shallots, sliced or chopped
1 cup white wine
½ cup sherry vinegar
¼ cup pepper jelly
1 teaspoon green curry paste
¼ cup loosely packed fresh basil leaves (save stems for cooking rice)
¼ cup loosely packed fresh cilantro leaves (save stems for cooking rice)
5-6 tablespoons unsalted butter
Salt
Fish sauce
Sambal oelek (Indonesian chili paste)

SHRIMP

2 egg whites
¼ cup sake
2 tablespoons cornstarch
Mixture of salt, cayenne, and Szechuan peppercorns
6 tablespoons olive or peanut oil
20 large shrimp (16-20 count)

To make sauce: In a small saucepan, combine shallots, wine, and sherry vinegar and bring to a boil. Reduce to ½ cup of liquid. Whisk in pepper jelly and remove from heat.

Pour into a blender. Add curry paste, basil, and cilantro and blend. Slowly blend in softened butter, 1 tablespoon at a time, until mixture is thick and creamy. Season with salt, fish sauce, and sambal oelek to taste. Keep warm.

To prepare shrimp: In a large bowl, whisk together egg whites, sake, cornstarch, and seasoning mixture. Toss shrimp in marinade and refrigerate for 1 hour.

Heat oil in a large skillet. Sauté shrimp in batches, for about 3 minutes. Drain and serve hot with the reserved sauce and Purple Rice (page 74).

This dish contains a variety of flavors that work well together. The pungency of cilantro and basil, the tang of vinegar, and the hot Asian pastes make for an intriguing sauce, especially when set against the sweetness of the shrimp.

Buckwheat Noodle Salad

Serves 4

3   tablespoons rice wine vinegar
1   tablespoon honey
½   teaspoon sambal oelek (Indonesian chili paste)
6   tablespoons peanut oil
½   pound buckwheat noodles
1   carrot

1   cucumber, halved and seeded
3   scallions
2   tablespoons chopped mint
2   tablespoons chopped peanuts (optional)
    Salt to taste
    Fresh lime juice to taste

To make dressing: In a small bowl, whisk together vinegar, honey, sambal oelek and oil. Set aside.

In a large saucepan, boil noodles. Drain noodles and plunge into ice water.

Drain and place in a bowl. Slice carrot, cucumber, and scallions into long strips. Add to noodles and toss with dressing and mint. Season to taste with salt and lime juice.

Purple Rice

Serves 4

3   cups water or broth, flavored with lemongrass, herb stems, and kefir lime leaves

½   pound Thai purple rice
½   cup coconut milk
    Salt

In a large saucepan, bring water or broth to a boil. Stir in rice and cover. Reduce heat and simmer for ½ hour, stirring from time to time. Rice will be almost creamy, like a risotto. Stir in coconut milk and salt to taste. Keep warm or serve immediately.

Gingerbread with Lime Cream

Serves 12

LIME CREAM

- 2 large eggs
- ½ cup sugar
- ⅓ cup fresh lime juice
  Zest of 1 lime, grated
- 4 tablespoons unsalted butter,
  cut into small pieces
- 2 cups whipping cream

GINGERBREAD

- 1 cup melted butter
- 1 cup sugar
- 3 large eggs
- 2 cups all-purpose flour
- 2 teaspoons baking soda
- 1 tablespoon grated fresh ginger
- 1 teaspoon ground cinnamon
- 1 teaspoon ground cloves
- 1 cup unsulphured molasses
- 2 teaspoons baking soda dissolved in
  2 tablespoons hot water

To make lime cream: In a medium-sized bowl, whip eggs and sugar at high speed with an electric beater, until double in volume and light in color. Mix in lime juice and zest.

Place in a double boiler over high heat and cook, whisking regularly, until very thick, about 20-30 minutes. Remove from heat and stir in butter. Strain and cool.

In a medium-sized bowl, whip cream into soft peaks. Fold into the lime cream and refrigerate until ready to serve.

To make gingerbread: Preheat oven to 350° F. Lightly grease a 9 x 13-inch baking pan.

Pour melted butter into a large bowl. Beat in sugar and eggs.

In a medium-sized bowl, sift together flour, cinnamon, cloves, and baking soda. Add ginger and mix briefly.

In a small bowl, mix molasses with the baking soda/hot water mixture and ½ cup boiling water. Whisk the dry mixture and then the wet mixture into the sugar and eggs. Bake 45-60 minutes. Cool on a rack. Cut into squares and top with lime cream.

75

Elizabeth Terry

W HEN I GOT MARRIED in 1966, my husband said to me, 'I know you're going to be a great cook.' He gave me two cookbooks: *A Treasury of Great Recipes* by Vincent Price and Dionne Lucas' menu cookbook. I didn't realize that cooking can be tricky, so I wasn't nervous about it at all. I just started on page one and made everything in both books . . . and that was my introduction to cooking." Elizabeth Terry spent the next fifteen years cooking only for friends and family. During that time she was also a parent, a probation officer, and worked at a wine and cheese shop before becoming a professional restaurateur. In 1981 Terry and her husband Michael opened Elizabeth's on 37th in Savannah, Georgia.

When they first moved to Savannah, Terry had planned to open a small lunch place, and her husband was going to practice law. Instead they found a building, a mansion, actually, and talked each other into opening a "real" restaurant, she says. This mansion houses the restaurant downstairs and the Terry family upstairs.

Terry has earned a reputation for offering gracious dining in an elegant setting. She describes the food at her restaurant as Southern cuisine with a historical reference. Most of the dishes are based on old Southern recipes and draw on indigenous ingredients such as pecans and sweet potatoes. In the coastal city of Savannah, seafood is a requisite, and crab, shrimp, and grouper are mainstays on the menu.

She describes a common occurrence at the restaurant—"When I go to the table, a lot of men pat me on the hand and say, 'Honey, you sure can cook!' I take it as a compliment, although other women might not."

Elizabeth Terry's background as a home cook and parent has made her very aware of the importance of nutrition, "I realize that food is the fuel for the body." Here, she has chosen a selection of savory dishes that reflect that philosophy and epitomize what comfort food is all about. Terry's user-friendly recipes featuring basic ingredients help us recapture a simpler time when life was less hectic.

Savannah Salad with Avocado Dressing

Serves 4

DRESSING

1 avocado, peeled, pitted, and diced
1 tablespoon cider vinegar
1 tablespoon fresh lemon juice
1 teaspoon minced garlic
½ teaspoon freshly ground black pepper
½ teaspoon salt
½ cup water

SALAD

6 cups mixed salad greens, washed, dried, and torn
2 oranges, peeled and diced
¼ cup chopped toasted pecans
2 tablespoons minced dried cranberries or raisins (optional)

A colorful salad featuring fruit and nut accents and a creamy dressing.

To make dressing: In a food processor, combine avocado, vinegar, lemon juice, garlic, pepper, salt, and water. Process until smooth, adding up to ¼ cup more water to make a dressing the consistency of heavy cream.

Note: the dressing must be made the day it is served or it will darken.

Just before serving, divide the greens among 4 salad plates. Spoon the dressing over and sprinkle each with oranges, pecans, and cranberries or raisins, if using.

Pepper-Pecan Brioche

Makes 1 loaf

This light brioche is a welcome addition to any breadbasket. Georgia pecans, in all their buttery richness, provide the perfect counterpoint to the bite of cracked peppercorns. I like to serve this brioche with fruit preserves.

1 tablespoon active dry yeast
1 tablespoon sugar
¼ cup lukewarm water
½ cup (1 stick) melted unsalted butter, cooled
½ teaspoon salt

2 cups all-purpose flour
⅓ cup pecans, toasted and chopped
1 teaspoon freshly cracked peppercorns
2 large eggs lightly beaten

In the bowl of a mixer, combine yeast, sugar, and water. Stir to dissolve. Allow the mixture to sit 10 minutes until bubbles form. Add butter, salt, flour, pecans, pepper, and eggs. Mix with the dough hook of the mixer or by hand with a wooden spoon until smooth, about 5 minutes.

Place the dough in a large buttered bowl and cover with a tea towel. Let rise until double in bulk, 1-1½ hours, no longer.

Lightly grease a loaf pan with butter.

Shape the dough and place in prepared loaf pan. Cover and allow to rise for one hour.

Preheat oven to 400° F.

Bake for 25 minutes or until golden. Remove from pan and cool.

Sweet Potatoes with Apple & Pear

Serves 4

The sweetness in this recipe complements chicken and pork dishes wonderfully.

3 cups peeled and diced sweet potatoes
½ teaspoon salt
2 bay leaves
1 apple, peeled and diced

1 pear, peeled and diced
½ cup apple cider
¼ teaspoon cinnamon
1 tablespoon sugar
2 tablespoons unsalted butter

In a medium saucepan bring the sweet potatoes, salt, and 1 cup water to a boil over high heat. Lower the heat, cover, and simmer until the potatoes are almost soft, about 6 minutes.

Stir in bay leaves, apple, pear, cider, cinnamon, sugar, and butter. Cover and simmer 10 more minutes. Remove the lid, stir, raise the heat to medium, and cook until the juice is reduced and slightly thickened, about 5 more minutes. Remove bay leaves and serve.

Roasted Thyme & Garlic-Spiced Cornish Hens

Serves 4

4   Cornish hens
3   tablespoons unsalted butter
2   tablespoons minced fresh thyme
2   tablespoons minced garlic

1   tablespoon cider vinegar
½   teaspoon freshly ground black
    pepper
½   teaspoon salt

Preheat oven to 400° F.

Rinse hens under cold water, pat dry, and set aside.

On a plate, using a fork, mash together butter, thyme, garlic, vinegar, pepper, and salt. Lift the skin from each side of the hen's breast and insert 2 teaspoons of flavored butter; 4 teaspoons per hen.

Place the hens on a roasting rack and bake for 45 minutes, or until juices run clear when pierced with fork.

A fresh herb butter spiked with vinegar bestows a special flavor to these tasty little birds. When served with fruit-enhanced sweet potatoes, you've got a complete comfort meal.

Tomatoes Stuffed with Spinach & Cheese

Serves 4

This classic flavor combination works with almost any entrée.

4 medium tomatoes
1 tablespoon extra virgin olive oil
8 ounces button mushrooms, wiped clean and diced
1 pound fresh spinach, stemmed, washed, dried, and chopped or chopped frozen spinach, thawed

1 tablespoon minced garlic
½ teaspoon freshly ground black pepper
½ cup grated cheddar cheese

Preheat oven to 400° F.

Slice about ½ inch off the top of tomatoes, remove core and seeds, and turn upside down on paper towel to drain.

In a large skillet, warm oil over high heat, then add mushrooms. Sauté until golden, about 3 minutes. Add garlic and spinach. Cover and cook until spinach is wilted, about 2 minutes. Remove from the heat, season with pepper, and toss with the cheese.

Stuff the reserved tomatoes with spinach mixture. Bake about 5 minutes, or until hot throughout.

Banana Pudding Parfait

Serves 4

¼ cup light Karo syrup	½ cup sugar
½ cup packed light brown sugar	2 tablespoons all-purpose flour
7 tablespoons unsalted butter	4 teaspoons cornstarch
¾ cup heavy cream	2 large eggs
2 tablespoons pure vanilla extract	2 cups warm milk
4 bananas, peeled and diced	

To make sauce: In a small saucepan, stir together Karo syrup, brown sugar, 1 tablespoon of the butter, and ¼ cup of the cream over medium heat. Bring to a boil, stirring constantly. Remove from heat. Cool 5 minutes, then stir in 1 tablespoon of the vanilla, and the bananas.

To make custard: In a large mixing bowl, whip together sugar, flour, cornstarch, and eggs until smooth and fluffy, about 3 minutes. Slowly pour in warm milk.

Pour custard mixture into a large saucepan and whisk over medium heat until it comes to a boil. Immediately remove from the heat and whisk in the remaining 6 tablespoons butter and the remaining tablespoon of vanilla.

To assemble: Spoon half the custard into 4 parfait glasses. Spoon in the banana caramel sauce, dividing evenly. Finish with the remaining custard. Chill the parfaits.

Just before serving, whip the remaining ½ cup cream into soft peaks and spoon over the parfaits.

This simple dessert is made with ingredients you likely have on hand. Sinfully rich with banana caramel sauce, custard, and whipped cream, it's reminiscent of a treat you would find at the ice cream parlors of yore.

Cindy Pawlcyn

"I NEVER REALLY WANTED to do anything else," says chef and restaurateur Cindy Pawlcyn. Her mother taught her to cook at an early age, but she says that her eyes opened to a new world of possibilities when a sister-in-law showed her how to cook Mexican food. It was simple and fun and quite different from anything she'd eaten growing up in Minnesota. By the time she was in high school, Pawlcyn was working five nights a week for a local catering company and taking cooking classes from a Cordon Bleu chef. Later, in cooking school, she was the only woman who wasn't planning to be a pastry chef or baker. After college she worked as sous-chef at several Chicago restaurants, including the renowned Pump Room, before moving to the Napa Valley.

Simplicity and fun seem to be two of Pawlcyn's watchwords. As executive chef and owner of six California restaurants, she is best known for her Fog City Diner, which opened in San Francisco in 1985. Pawlcyn is often credited with reinventing diner food in a playful setting. That concept has proved so successful that she has recently opened Fog City Diners in Dallas, Las Vegas, and Chattanooga. Her excitement and enthusiasm for her work are unmistakable. These days she devotes a good deal of time to working with her chefs "to fine-tune their food and make their dishes more palatable and more organized and more delicious," she says.

Pawlcyn describes her food as straightforward and healthy, although "I probably use a little too much butter to be truly healthy. I try to keep the food unintimidating, even though I might be using obscure and bizarre ingredients."

Here, Pawlcyn presents a menu of Spanish tapas—appetizers customarily served with drinks at Spanish bars. This concept has evolved to give diners a taste of a variety of dishes at one meal. She sees this meal as "an in-front-of-the-fire kind of dinner with close friends. There would be many different foods served from a communal table on small plates, with a selection of sherries or wines." Pawlcyn seems to have a lively anecdote for each recipe. The Snails in Spicy Sauce come from her travels in Spain. "We had a stopover in a home near Segovia to have a bite and some champagne with local dignitaries known by our host," she says. "As we were leaving, their son met us with a beautiful casserole of tiny snails and a shot glass of toothpicks— we just stood by the front door and gorged ourselves. It was heaven!"

Snails in Spicy Sauce

Serves 6-8

3 tablespoons olive oil
1 onion, finely chopped
4 cloves garlic, minced
1 red bell pepper, minced
1 green bell pepper, minced
1 ancho chili, minced
3-4 ounces minced chorizo

2 teaspoons sweet paprika
1 branch fresh thyme
2 bay leaves
2 tablespoons tomato paste
1 cup dry red wine
80 small snails

In a large sauté pan, heat oil. Add onions, peppers, and chili, and sauté until tender. Add chorizo and cook until crispy. Add paprika, thyme, bay leaves, and tomato paste, and cook 1 minute more. Add wine and bring to a boil. Reduce heat to low, add snails, and simmer until heated through.

These delectable morsels may be served with grilled garlic bread, or stuffed into the hearts of artichokes, popped back into the oven until hot and bubbly, and served as a first course.

℮ℵ

Tortilla Español

Serves 6-8

2 tablespoons olive oil
2 small onions, minced
3 medium Yukon Gold or Yellow Finn potatoes (approximately 1-1½ pounds) steamed in their jackets, sliced into circles

¼ teaspoon minced fresh thyme
3 tablespoons minced fresh parsley
5 large eggs
3 tablespoons water
Salt & freshly ground black pepper
1 teaspoon paprika

Preheat oven to 350° F.

In a large, ovenproof, nonstick pan, heat oil. Add all but 2 tablespoons of the onions and sauté until soft. Add potatoes, thyme, and 1 tablespoon of the parsley. Mix well. Cook slowly.

Meanwhile, beat eggs with water. Season with salt and pepper. Pour eggs over potato and onion mixture. Stir a bit and place in oven. Bake about 10 minutes or until set.

Flip tortilla onto a serving platter. Garnish with paprika and the remaining 2 tablespoons of the parsley and 2 tablespoons of the onions.

This dish can be served room temperature or hot.

For the uninitiated, I recommend the oven, but I always do this dish on the stovetop. (It impresses my stepkids to watch me flip the tortilla.) Try to find true Spanish paprika, which has a nice smoky aroma and flavor.

℮ℵ

Shrimp in Garlic Sauce

Serves 6-8

- ¼ cup olive oil
- 6 cloves garlic, peeled and crushed
- 2 tablespoons finely minced shallots
- 1-2 dried pequin chilies, seeded, whole or chopped
- 8 bay leaves
- 1 pound shrimp in shells, split and deveined
- ⅛-¼ teaspoon salt
- 1 tablespoon minced parsley
- Juice of 1 lemon

In a shallow earthenware casserole, heat oil over low heat. Add garlic, shallots, chilies, and bay leaves. Cook until garlic and shallots are golden, about 5 minutes. Add shrimp and salt; cook, covered, stirring occasionally, 10-15 minutes. (Cooking time will depend on the size of shrimp you use.) Sprinkle with parsley and lemon juice.

This dish tastes best if you can use fresh shrimp. It's also great with crayfish tails or crab.

Pimentos à la Malagueña

Serves 6-8

- 6 small pimentos or 3 red bell peppers
- 3 tablespoons olive oil
- 1 small onion, chopped
- 1 clove garlic, chopped
- ¼ cup Malaga or other raisins

Roast the peppers over an open flame or under the broiler until charred. Transfer to a bowl, cover with plastic wrap, and let cool. When cool, peel and cut into wide strips, saving any juice.

In a large sauté pan, heat oil. Add onions and garlic, and sauté until soft. Add raisins and cook until they are plump. Add the reserved peppers. Cook to heat through.

These roasted peppers are great with meat or poultry or on their own as a tapa. If you can't find the Malaga raisins, use golden raisins. I serve this with plenty of grilled semolina bread or olive bread.

Fried Almonds

Serves 6-8

2 cups almonds with skins on
1-1½ cups olive oil

Kosher salt to taste

In a large, heavy skillet over medium heat, heat oil and almonds, stirring until toasted. Drain on a paper towel. Salt immediately.

Bay-Infused Crème Caramel

Serves 6-8

½ cup sugar
   Juice of ½ lemon
1 teaspoon water
10 bay leaves (French or Russian)
4 cups half-and-half

4 egg yolks
2 large eggs
⅓ cup sugar
   Tiny pinch of salt

To make caramel: Have 6-8 custard cups handy.

   In a small saucepan, combine sugar, lemon juice, and water. Boil, stirring, until a rich, golden brown. Pour equal amounts into the bottoms of custard cups; swirl to coat sides with caramel. Use caution, as caramel is extremely hot. Set aside.

   To make custard: Lightly toast bay leaves by holding in tongs over gas flame for 1 or 2 seconds, or heat in small, dry pan until aroma rises.

   Preheat oven to 325° F.

   In a large saucepan, combine bay leaves and half-and-half. Simmer 15 minutes, gently swirling pan so that half-and-half heats evenly. Do not whisk—air would make custard rubbery. Remove from heat and cool slightly. Remove the bay leaves.

   In a medium-sized mixing bowl, whisk yolks, eggs, sugar, and salt together. Whisk in the warm half-and-half. Strain into the prepared custard cups and place in a pan filled with enough warm water to reach halfway up the custard cups. Cover with foil. Bake 40-45 minutes or until custard is set. When cool, run knife around edge of cup and invert onto dish to serve.

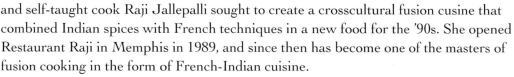

Raji Jallepalli

W HEN I WOULD GO to Indian restaurants, nothing remarkable happened on the plate. And to me the food has to be the star. At French restaurants the emphasis is on presentation, texture, and freshness. But I always felt that French restaurant food could stand lightening up a bit and could benefit from some more assertive flavors and bouquets." Based on these observations, the former microbiologist and self-taught cook Raji Jallepalli sought to create a crosscultural fusion cuisine that combined Indian spices with French techniques in a new food for the '90s. She opened Restaurant Raji in Memphis in 1989, and since then has become one of the masters of fusion cooking in the form of French-Indian cuisine.

"The French-Indian premise is so new and uncharted it will take me years to experiment with everything I want to try." Indeed, reading Jallepalli's menu might send the uninitiated running to the food dictionary, and wondering how one meal with dishes like spice-crusted tuna with sesame turmeric emulsion, beef tenderloin with wild mushroom reduction, cranberry beurre noir and toasted fenugreek, and crustillant of crab with razorback caviar and blackberry chutney might go together. But that is exactly the sophisticated type of menu served at Raji. The kitchen has become her laboratory and she has created a unique brand of culinary alchemy where every ingredient shines and each dish is designed to complement the other.

Jallepalli uses very little cream or butter—she generally prefers fruit and vegetable purees and emulsions to creamy sauces, although she does create some very special fusion beurre blancs. "My cooking is complex in flavors, but it really is not complicated. I want the bouquet to be simple and subtle." She offers several interesting observations on ingredients. She has found that shallots don't translate well into fusion cooking because of their sharper taste, so she tends to use onions instead. One ingredient that creates real depth in fusion cooking is olive oil, Jallepalli says. She uses it as a catalyst that makes a reaction.

Jallepalli counts chefs Jean Louis Palladin and Daniel Boulud among those who have been instrumental in molding her career. "They've inspired me in the approach they take to food, in the serious attitude they take toward food, and in the possibilities that can be conceived."

In this menu Jallepalli gives us a whole new spectrum of possibilities in one meal. As at her restaurant, she presents a degustation, or tasting menu, featuring small portions of a variety of dishes, in this case seafood, game, and pork—crowned with a transcendent crème brûlée.

$\mathscr{S}$hrimp Wrapped in Phyllo Pastry with Tomato Coulis

Serves 8

FILLING

- 3 tablespoons canola oil
- ½ teaspoon mustard seeds
- 1½ cups finely chopped cabbage
- 1 pinch turmeric
  Salt

COULIS

- 4 tablespoons olive oil
- 10 medium Roma tomatoes, peeled, seeded, and chopped
- ½ teaspoon turmeric

- ¼ teaspoon cayenne pepper
- ¼ teaspoon cumin
  Salt

SHRIMP & PASTRY

- 1 pound colossal shrimp (U6 or U10 size) cleaned, shelled, and deveined
  Salt
- 1 pinch macerated cumin seeds

- 8 sheets phyllo dough (9 x 13-inch size)
- ¼ cup (½ stick) butter, melted

To make filling: In a large skillet, heat oil over high heat, add mustard seeds and sauté until seeds pop. Add cabbage, turmeric, and salt to taste; sauté just until al dente, about 1-2 minutes. Remove from heat and set aside.

To make coulis: In a large skillet, heat oil over high heat. Add tomatoes, turmeric, cayenne pepper, cumin, and salt to taste. Cook until tomatoes are soft and stewy, about 5-10 minutes. Remove from heat. Cool for 5 minutes. In a blender or food processor, blend into a fine puree. Set aside.

To prepare shrimp: Salt shrimp lightly and toss with cumin seeds.

To prepare pastry: Keep phyllo dough covered with plastic wrap so it won't turn brittle. Cut a sheet of phyllo into three 3-inch strips. Brush a light layer of butter over the entire surface of one strip, starting

(continued on next page)

(Shrimp Wrapped in Phyllo Pastry continued)

first with the edges. Set a second sheet of phyllo on top of the first, brush with butter, and repeat process with a third sheet and set aside. Repeat this procedure with the remaining 7 sheets of phyllo until you have assembled 8 stacks.

To assemble: Preheat the oven to 400° F. On a work surface, place the 8 stacks of the prepared phyllo pastry. Place one of the shrimp and 2 tablespoons of cabbage filling on each phyllo stack. Wrap tightly, folding a 1-inch strip over the head of the shrimp. Brush the outside lightly with the remaining melted butter. Bake for 10 minutes or until golden crisp.

Spoon ⅛ cup of the tomato coulis into a circle on each plate. Place the wrapped shrimp, with its tail up, on the coulis.

Fillet of Rainbow Trout with Lemon-Lime Beurre Blanc

Serves 8

We get wonderful rainbow trout in Tennessee. The lemon-lime beurre blanc is subtle enough to allow the flavor of the fish to come through. Ajowan is a spice in the fennel family, and has a nice bite to it.

ॐ

BEURRE BLANC
- 1 tablespoon canola oil
- 4 tablespoons chopped onion
- 1½ cups whipping cream
- 1 pinch turmeric
-   Salt
- 1 quarter lemon, seeded
- 1 quarter lime, seeded
- ¼ cup white wine
- ¼ teaspoon ajowan powder (may substitute ground fennel seeds)

VEGETABLES & TROUT
- 6 tablespoons canola oil
- 1 medium-sized summer squash, diced into 1-inch cubes
- 2 bunches spinach, stemmed, washed, and dried
-   Salt
- 8 rainbow trout fillets
-   Ajowan powder
- 1 cup unsalted butter or canola oil

To make sauce: In a medium-sized saucepan heat oil over medium heat. Add onions and cook until soft. Increase heat, add cream, turmeric, and salt to taste and bring to boil. As sauce begins to reduce, squeeze in lemon and lime juice and toss in the peels. Add wine and ajowan powder. Let sauce reduce for a few minutes. Cool for 15 minutes. Strain, discarding rinds. Keep warm.

To make vegetables: In a large skillet heat 3 tablespoons of the oil over high heat. Add summer squash; sauté until tender. Remove from the pan. Keep warm. In the same pan, heat the remaining 3 tablespoons of oil. Add spinach and sauté, stirring until just wilted. Remove from heat. Add salt to taste and toss the reserved squash back into the spinach. Keep warm.

To prepare trout: Sprinkle trout lightly with salt and a dash of ajowan powder. In a large skillet over medium heat melt 2 tablespoons butter or oil for each fillet to be cooked. Add the trout and cook, turning once, for about 2 minutes. Trout cooks very fast; it is important not to overcook. Brush the skin lightly with butter.

To serve: Place about ⅛ cup sauce, spread as thinly as possible, on each of 8 plates. Place a portion of the warm spinach-squash mixture across the middle of each plate as a base for the trout. Place a trout fillet atop each plate of spinach.

Quail Salad with Tandoori Spices & Grilled Corn

Serves 8

4 ears corn
Salt
10 tablespoons olive oil, plus extra for corn

2 tablespoons tandoori spices
8 semi-boneless quail
2 tablespoons balsamic vinegar
8 handfuls mesclun greens

On a grill or a gas burner, grill corn until brown. Cut kernels from cobs, mix with a pinch of salt and enough olive oil just to coat lightly, and set aside.

Combine 6 tablespoons of the olive oil and tandoori spices. Rub quail with this mixture. In a skillet, sear the quail over high heat, and cook until juices run clear, about 8-10 minutes. Remove from heat and keep warm.

Whisk together vinegar and the remaining 4 tablespoons olive oil. Toss greens in the vinaigrette.

To assemble: Bunch greens into small bouquets on each plate, top with 2-3 tablespoons grilled corn, and place a quail on top of each salad.

Indian spices, grilled corn, and the meat of a delicate game bird combine to make a delicious salad. You should have your butcher remove the back and rib cage of the quail, leaving the wings and legs.

ଏ

Tenderloin of Pork
with Curried Blueberry Sauce

Serves 8

I don't use the traditional Madras curry powder in many dishes, but in this pork tenderloin recipe it blends perfectly with the other ingredients.

4 tablespoons (½ stick) unsalted butter
2 cups fresh blueberries
  Salt
  Heavy cream (optional)
1 teaspoon curry powder
2 tablespoons finely chopped fresh ginger

1 teaspoon ground coriander
½ teaspoon red pepper
  Scant amount canola oil to sear pork
3 4-ounce pork tenderloins
¼ cup canola oil
2 pounds assorted mushrooms, diced into 1-inch cubes
  Indian curry leaves (optional)

In a medium-sized saucepan, melt butter over medium heat. Add blueberries and salt to taste; cook until the berries are soft, about 10 minutes. Transfer to a food processor or blender, blend into a smooth puree; if necessary, add a bit of cream to make the texture smooth.

Return the mixture to the saucepan and bring to a boil. Remove from heat. Strain. Stir in curry powder.

Preheat the oven to 350° F.

In a small bowl, mix ginger, coriander, and red pepper. Rub pork with the spice mixture.

In a large, ovenproof skillet, heat oil over medium-high heat, add the pork and sear on both sides to seal in the juices. Place skillet in oven and roast for 8-10 minutes.

In a large skillet, heat ¼ cup canola oil over medium heat. Add mushrooms and curry leaves, and sauté until lightly browned, about 5 minutes. Add salt to taste.

Paint each plate with the warm blueberry sauce. Place a portion of mushrooms in the center of each plate. Slice the pork and place two slices on top of the mushrooms.

Mango Crème Brûlée

Serves 8

---

4 cups whipping cream	2 tablespoons ground cardamom
12 egg yolks	¼ cup toasted coconut
1 cup sugar	4 tablespoons packed brown sugar
1 cup mango sauce	

Preheat oven to 350° F.

In a large saucepan over high heat, cook cream until just scalded. Remove from heat.

In a large bowl, beat egg yolks for 1 minute at medium speed. Add the scalded cream, sugar, mango sauce, and 1 tablespoon of the cardamom powder. Mix well. Pour mixture into ramekins.

Place ramekins in a water bath and bake 30-40 minutes, or until custard is set.

In a food processor, process toasted coconut until powderlike. Set aside.

Divide 2 tablespoons of the brown sugar over the top of each custard. Place under the broiler until the sugar is just caramelized.

In a small bowl, mix toasted coconut, the remaining 1 tablespoon of the cardamom, and the remaining 2 tablespoons of the brown sugar. Sprinkle atop the custards and serve warm.

A harmonious dish that reflects the true fusion concept. Mango from the tropics and cardamom from India are used to create the quintessentially French custard.

Lidia Bastianich

S HE IS WIDELY CONSIDERED to be the doyenne of Italian cuisine in the United States. As chef and co-owner of three New York restaurants, a cookbook writer, and food historian, Lidia Bastianich has been instrumental in bringing authentic Italian cooking to the American public. She has had a long-standing love affair with food. "I love to touch food. I love to prepare it. It's the medium that I communicate best in." This very special form of communication has transported New Yorkers to epicurean heights for years.

She first took an interest in the food of her native Italy as a young child. Her grandparents ran an inn and produced all their own food— Bastianich says she remembers it all, from sausage-making to milking the goat. When her family immigrated to New York City in 1958, Bastianich gravitated toward part-time jobs in bakeries and restaurants. Although she expected to study science at Hunter College, she returned to culinary pursuits permanently after she met her husband, Felice, who was a maître d'. The couple opened their first restaurant in 1971. Bastianich says she didn't consider herself a professional cook at the time, so she hired a chef and worked beside him. She discovered that she could indeed cook—better than the hired professional. After two years she took charge of the kitchen.

In 1981 the Bastianiches opened Felidia, specializing in the regional flavors of northeastern Italy. Bastianich is from Istria, near the Yugoslavian border, an area influenced by the Slavic cultures. So although she characterizes her food as Italian, she has developed a unique style she refers to as "border cuisine," incorporating ingredients like sauerkraut, beans, lots of potatoes, dumplings, spaetzle, and strudel into her dishes. These unusual cultural combinations have become a trademark. "Food for me is really the protagonist. I can only transport or exalt it," she says. "The product is 50 percent or more of what I do. I have to embellish it or bring it out or dress it up a little bit—as simply as I can." As she speaks, it becomes clear that with her love of food comes a real sense of responsibility to give her customers just the right thing.

For the Bastianiches, food is a family affair. Lidia's son, Joseph, is involved with the new restaurants, Becco and Frico, which continue to honor the distinctive origins of true Italian cooking. And for Lidia, her restaurants are much more than a business; they are what she calls "the expression of our family's shared memories, experiences, traditions, and cultural heritage, our desire to share with others what has been handed down to us over generations."

Crabmeat & Leek Soup

Serves 6

4 tablespoons extra virgin olive oil
3 large potatoes, peeled and diced
  Salt & freshly ground black pepper
  Ground red pepper
2 leeks, washed, trimmed, and cut into thin strips
4 scallions, washed, trimmed, and cut into thin strips

4 fresh bay leaves
4 quarts chicken or vegetable stock, heated
1 pound skate, skin and cartilage removed, and cut into 1-inch pieces
10 ounces Dungeness crab or king crab

In a large skillet heat oil. Add potatoes and cook until browned. Stir in salt, black pepper, and red pepper to taste. Add leeks, scallions, and bay leaves. Stir just until wilted. Add hot stock. Bring to a boil, reduce heat to low, adjust seasonings to taste, and simmer for 30 minutes.

Add skate; cook 10 minutes more. Add crab and cook another 10 minutes.

Remove bay leaves before serving.

My Uncle Emilio was an electrician by profession, but a fisherman at heart. We lived near the fish market, and when he did not sell all of his night's catch, he would bring the fish to our home. I remember the spiny crabs — still alive when my uncle would let them loose in the bathtub. Dinner on those days was always very special, and this soup is a part of those memories.

Rigatoni in a Woodman Sauce

Serves 6

3 tablespoons olive oil

½ cup chopped onion

¼ pound sweet Italian sausage, removed from casing

2 tablespoons unsalted butter

2 cups sliced mushrooms, mixed varieties

1 cup canned peeled Italian tomatoes, crushed

½ cup fresh ricotta cheese

1 cup cooked fresh peas, or frozen

1 cup half-and-half
   Salt & freshly ground black pepper

1 pound rigatoni

1 cup freshly grated Parmigiano-Reggiano cheese

In a large nonreactive saucepan, heat oil over moderate heat. Add onions and cook until soft, about 3 minutes. Add sausage and cook, stirring, for 10 minutes. Drain the fat from the pan. Add butter and mushrooms and cook for 3 minutes. Add tomatoes and simmer gently until thick, about 10 minutes. Add ¼ cup of ricotta to the sauce and mix well, then add peas and half-and-half. Boil lightly until thick and creamy, about 4 minutes. Season with salt and pepper to taste.

Cook rigatoni in a large pot of boiling salted water until al dente. Drain well. Add the pasta to the sauce and mix well over low heat. Fold in Parmigiano-Reggiano and the remaining ¼ cup ricotta.

This is a comforting mellow dish with an earthy essence that comes from the mushrooms.

String Beans & Potatoes

Serves 6

2 medium-to-large Idaho potatoes

1 pound fresh string beans, trimmed

3 tablespoons olive oil

4 cloves garlic, sliced

¼ teaspoon salt
   Freshly ground black pepper

Boil potatoes for 20 minutes in 2 quarts of salted water. Add beans and boil until the vegetables are just tender, 7 minutes longer. Strain through a colander, discarding the liquid. Remove the potatoes and set aside. Refresh the beans under cold water and drain well.

When the potatoes are cool enough to handle, peel and slice them ⅓-inch thick. If the beans are long, halve them crosswise.

In a deep skillet, heat olive oil. Add garlic and sauté until golden. Add potatoes and beans to skillet. Season with salt, and pepper to taste. Mash potatoes coarsely. Mix together well.

In Istria, the combination of potatoes with many green vegetables is part of the culinary culture. Swiss chard and potatoes, savoy cabbage and potatoes, spinach and potatoes—all can basically be prepared in the same fashion.

Swordfish in a Sweet & Sour Sauce

Serves 6

6 8-ounce skinless swordfish steaks
   Salt & freshly ground black pepper
   Flour for dredging and browning
6 tablespoons vegetable oil
3 tablespoons small marinated capers

1 cup white wine
1 cup balsamic vinegar
1 tablespoon olive oil
1 tablespoon unsalted butter
   (optional)

Lightly salt and pepper the fish, and dredge each piece in flour, shaking off excess. In a large nonreactive skillet, heat the vegetable oil over high heat. Add the fish and sauté about 1½ minutes on each side until browned and cooked through, 4-5 minutes per side in all. Transfer to a platter, cover with aluminum foil, and keep warm.

   Drain oil from skillet. Return the skillet to medium heat, add a pinch of flour, and let it brown briefly. Add capers, wine, vinegar, olive oil, and butter. Increase the heat to high and boil, shaking the pan, until sauce is thickened to a light syrup, about 4 minutes. Spoon sauce over swordfish and serve immediately.

Note: If you like your fish well done, return the fish to the sauce and cook an additional minute before serving.

Balsamic vinegar is an ingredient that makes any dish speak Italian—so why not use it with swordfish? This traditional Sicilian dish, Pesce Spada in Agrodolce, marries swordfish, vinegar, and capers.

Apple Strudel

Serves 6-8

Istria was under Austro-Hungarian rule around the turn of the century, and its cuisine was influenced by this occupation. Certainly this Strudel Di Mele is a Middle European specialty.

DOUGH
- 2 cups sifted all-purpose flour
- ½ teaspoon salt
- 3 tablespoons oil

FILLING
- ½ cup (1 stick) unsalted butter
- 1 cup dried, unflavored breadcrumbs
- ½ teaspoon cinnamon

- 1½ cups sugar
- 3 pounds green apples, such as Granny Smith
  Grated zest and juice of 1 lemon
- 1 cup raisins, soaked in 2 tablespoons rum for 30 minutes
  Oil for preparing baking sheet and brushing the strudel
  Confectioners' sugar for dusting

To make dough: In a large mixing bowl, make a well with flour, add salt and oil, and slowly mix with as much tepid water as needed to make a silky dough. Knead dough well, then allow it to rest for 45 minutes in a warm place covered with a damp towel.

To make filling: In a medium-sized sauté pan melt ¼ cup butter over medium heat. Add breadcrumbs, stirring continuously until lightly toasted, about 5 minutes. Remove from heat and mix in cinnamon and ½ cup of the sugar. Set aside.

Peel, core, and slice apples. Place them in a large bowl and add the remaining sugar, lemon rind and juice, and rum-soaked raisins. Mix well and set aside.

To assemble: Preheat oven to 450° F. Lightly coat a baking sheet with oil. Roll out dough into a very thin rectangle (approximately 18 x 12 inches) with the longer sides facing you. The dough should be very elastic; you should be able to pull and stretch it with your hands.

Place a kitchen towel or cheesecloth

along the far side of the dough.

Spread the breadcrumb mixture evenly over the dough, leaving a clean 1½-inch border on each side. Dot the breadcrumbs with small pieces of the remaining ¼ cup butter.

Make a long mound of the apple mixture on top of the breadcrumbs along the side closest to you, leaving the 1½-inch border clean.

Begin rolling as you would a jelly roll until all the dough has been rolled, finishing on a kitchen towel or cheesecloth.

Seal the ends by folding over the dough and pressing with your fingers. Transfer the strudel from the towel or cheesecloth to the prepared baking sheet by placing it diagonally, or if too long, shape it into a horseshoe.

Brush strudel lightly with olive oil and place in preheated oven. Immediately lower the temperature to 375° F, and bake for 1 hour. If top begins to brown too much, lower temperature to 350° F.

Cool on a rack. Sprinkle with confectioners' sugar.

Cornmeal Cookies

Makes about 6 dozen

1½ cups all-purpose flour
1 cup fine yellow cornmeal
1 teaspoon baking powder
½ teaspoon salt
¾ cup (1½ sticks) unsalted butter
⅔ cup sugar

1 large egg
2 teaspoons grated lemon zest
1 teaspoon pure vanilla extract
¾ cup golden raisins, soaked in ¼ cup warm water

Preheat the oven to 375° F. Lightly butter and flour two baking sheets.

In a medium-sized bowl, combine flour, cornmeal, baking powder, and salt.

In a large bowl, beat together butter and sugar until fluffy. Beat in the egg. Add lemon zest and vanilla and blend well. Add the dry ingredients, mix well, then add raisins and water and stir until combined. Chill for 1 hour.

Roll out dough to a ¼-inch thickness. Cut the dough into 1½-inch-long diamond shapes. Place the cookies on the prepared baking sheets and bake for 12-15 minutes. Transfer to wire racks to cool.

In Venetian dialect "Zalo" means "giallo" or yellow, and these Zaletti—yellow cookies—take precisely that color from the cornmeal that is used in their preparation.

Gale Gand

THE LAST THING Gale Gand's parents wanted was for their daughter to become a chef. Gand's mother, a skilled baker herself, felt that if Gale learned domestic or typing skills, she would forever be relegated to "woman's work." So Gand pursued the arts, studying silver- and goldsmithing in college. But two incidents changed her career path. One night she was enlisted to help in the kitchen at her favorite vegetarian restaurant when the chef didn't show up. Despite her total lack of cooking experience she was immediately captivated by the sensory and creative aspects of dealing with food.

An outing to a fancy restaurant in Cleveland was the next formative incident. It was a prix fixe menu and she thought it was wonderful to eat a succession of courses in an elegant setting. Gand became obsessed with the idea of working in this restaurant. "It was like falling in love, I couldn't get it out of my mind. I wanted to be part of that environment." She dropped out of school for a year to work at Au Provence as a waitress since she didn't have the credentials to work in the kitchen. The restaurant had a huge library and Gand would spend hours there reading cookbooks. That year convinced her that she had found a new art form to pursue.

Gand started a catering company and cooked at several restaurants. Curious to see if an American woman could be accepted in the kitchens of restaurants in France, she contacted all the three-star restaurants there in search of an apprenticeship. All but one said no. When she arrived at the restaurant in Lyons and announced herself as Gale Gand, she was met with puzzled looks and shaking heads. No, she was told, they were expecting a *Mr.* Gale Gand. Once both sides got over their initial shock, Gand settled right in to the all-male kitchen and says she learned more there than in any other cooking experience.

Gand and her husband, chef Rick Tramonto, have opened thirteen restaurants together, including Bice and Bella Luna in Chicago. They were hired to transform the kitchen and cuisine of the Stapleford Park Hotel outside London, which gave them the opportunity to live and work in England, France, and Spain. While living in England, Gand discovered that most English wheat doesn't make good bread. Undaunted, she found a miller who would grind the type of flour she needed to bake her singular pastries and breads.

Gand and Tramonto are currently cooking rustic French, Italian, and American food at their new restaurant, Brasserie T, outside Chicago. Gand describes the simple, hearty fare as "familiar dishes turned inside out," and says they are doing a lot of slow cooking and roasting to bring out the fullest flavor of their ingredients. This simple supper is perfect for the fall and winter months.

Butternut Squash Soup

Serves 4-6

2 tablespoons unsalted butter
1 medium Spanish onion, diced
4 butternut squash, peeled and cubed
¼ cup pecans
6 cups chicken stock

1 pinch freshly grated nutmeg
  Salt & freshly ground white pepper
1 tablespoon grated Parmesan cheese
1 tablespoon crushed amaretti
2 teaspoons chopped chives

In a large stockpot, melt butter over medium heat. Add onions and cook until transparent. Add squash and pecans and continue cooking to toast nuts. Add chicken stock and simmer until squash is tender, about 20 minutes.

In a food processor or blender, puree the soup, then season to taste. Ladle into bowls and sprinkle with cheese, crushed cookies, and chives.

I love the subtle, sweet flavor of butternut squash; it makes a great pureed soup. The pecans add a nutty taste while the amaretto cookies add contrast in texture.

Red Onion Focaccia

Serves 4-6

1¼ cups mashed potatoes
⅝ cup milk, warmed
2½ cups all-purpose flour
1 tablespoon kosher salt, plus extra for top

⅓ cup rosemary olive oil plus ¼ cup for topping
2 tablespoons garlic oil
1½ tablespoons yeast
¼ red onion, sliced

Grease a 14 x 12-inch sheet pan.

In a medium-sized saucepan warm potatoes and milk over medium heat, stirring. Place in a mixer with a dough hook. Add flour, 1 tablespoon salt, ⅓ cup rosemary olive oil, garlic oil, yeast, and onions. Mix on low speed for 6 minutes, or knead by hand for 10 minutes, or until smooth.

Oil the top of dough. Let rise until dough is double in bulk. Roll out on a floured surface and placed on greased pan. Pierce dough over entire surface, then coat with ¼ cup additional rosemary olive oil and let rise till doubled in height.

Preheat oven to 400° F. Sprinkle dough with salt and bake about 20 minutes, until golden brown.

Potato & Goat Cheese Salad with Bacon Vinaigrette

Serves 4

VINAIGRETTE

½ cup red wine vinegar
1 clove garlic, minced and sautéed
1 large shallot, chopped and sautéed
1 tablespoon brown sugar
½ cup olive oil
    Salt & freshly ground black pepper
¼ pound bacon, cooked and crumbled

SALAD

8 red potatoes, boiled and sliced
1 medium oven-roasted Vidalia onion, chopped
2 cups crumbled goat cheese
6 ounces frisée
2 teaspoons chopped chives
2 plum tomatoes, seeded and chopped
½ cup sliced cucumber
    Fresh herbs for garnish, such as rosemary, thyme, or basil

Here's a contemporary twist on German potato salad—it's one of my favorite salads.

To make vinaigrette: Whisk together vinegar, garlic, shallots, and brown sugar. Add oil in a slow stream, whisk until emulsified. Season to taste. Stir in chopped bacon.

To make salad: Toss potatoes and onions with ½ cup of the vinaigrette. Warm in the oven or microwave, then keep warm on a serving platter. In a medium-sized bowl, combine tomatoes, goat cheese, frisée, cucumbers, and chives. Add the remaining vinaigrette and toss. Place salad mixture on top of the potato and onion mixture. Drizzle with some additional vinaigrette. Garnish with fresh herbs.

Sautéed Salmon
with Barley & Lentil Risotto

Serves 4

This salmon couldn't be easier to prepare. A creamy legume risotto makes for a flavorful pairing.

RISOTTO
- 4 tablespoons unsalted butter
- 2 shallots, minced
- ½ cup Arborio rice
- ½ cup barley
- ½ cup green lentils
- 2-4 cups chicken stock, boiling
- ½ cup Parmesan cheese
- 3 tablespoons whipped cream
- Salt & freshly ground black pepper
- 1 teaspoon fresh herbs, chopped

SALMON
- 4 6-ounce salmon fillets
- Salt & freshly ground black pepper
- 2 tablespoons roasted garlic oil

To make risotto: In a large sauté pan, melt 2 tablespoons of the butter over medium heat. Add shallots and cook until transparent. Add rice and sauté to coat. Add barley and lentils. Begin to add stock, a ladle at a time, stirring constantly. When stock is absorbed, add another ladle. Continue adding stock while cooking until rice and grains are tender, about 30 minutes. Stir in Parmesan and the remaining 2 tablespoons of butter to create a creamy mixture. Fold in whipped cream, salt and pepper to taste, and herbs.

To prepare salmon: Season salmon with salt and pepper. In a sauté pan, heat garlic oil and sauté fish for about 3-4 minutes on each side, or until desired doneness. Serve with risotto.

Blueberry Bread & Butter Pudding

Serves 6

1 loaf brioche	6 eggs
2 cups half-and-half	1 cup sugar
2 cups heavy cream	1 pint blueberries
1 pinch salt	Confectioners' sugar for topping
1 vanilla bean, split	

Preheat oven to 350° F.

Remove crust from brioche and cut the loaf into cubes. Place cubes on a baking sheet and toast in oven until golden brown.

In a saucepan, heat half-and-half, cream, salt, and vanilla bean just until boiling. Remove from heat and allow vanilla to infuse.

Meanwhile, in a large stainless steel bowl, whisk together eggs and sugar. Slowly add hot cream mixture, whisking constantly to make a custard. Strain the mixture through a fine sieve.

Toss brioche cubes with custard and let them soak. Sprinkle berries into the bottom of 6 small baking dishes. Divide soaked bread among the dishes and top with any remaining custard.

Place dishes in a water bath and bake for 25-30 minutes, until set and golden brown. Sprinkle with confectioners' sugar.

This dessert was inspired by my time living in England, where the entire cuisine seems to be based on bread.

Patty Queen

THIS THIRD-GENERATION CHEF says she cannot remember a time in her life spent away from a professional kitchen. Patty Queen's Polish immigrant grandfather brought Connecticut its first diner. Her mother ran the family catering business in which Queen grew up. Cooking is the only career she ever considered. Today, she and her brother own and operate The Cottage Restaurant outside Hartford, Connecticut.

After graduating from Johnson and Wales College in Rhode Island in 1986 with a degree in culinary arts, Queen moved to Boston, where her first cooking experience was at the Harvest Restaurant in Cambridge. There, unusual ingredients and preparations were an everyday affair. She remembers, "There was this wild guy training me. He said, 'We're going to do a duck confit salad with some kind of greens and a huckleberry vinaigrette.' I didn't have any idea what he was talking about! At the end of the night there were twenty-five items coming off of my station." This intense first professional cooking experience taught her to think on her feet and to be creative, and landed her a job as line cook at the renowned Restaurant Jasper. She counts Jasper White and Julia Child, a frequent patron at Jasper's, among her influences.

Wanting to expand her food horizons, Queen decided to treat herself to six months of "culinary finishing school" in Europe. To experience the origins of American food, her research took her to Paris, Rome, Burgundy, Bordeaux, London, and Amsterdam. When her funds ran out after two months, she took a job as a chef in Florence. Unfortunately, the turmoil caused in Europe by the Gulf War in 1991 prompted an early return to the States.

In 1992 Queen moved to New Orleans to work at The Bistro at Maison de Ville. She eventually became executive chef, following in Susan Spicer's footsteps.

Queen's European experience certainly informed her approach to food. She insists that her "imaginative contemporary" cuisine must start with the freshest seasonal and regional ingredients. Spontaneity is important too: "If I had to stop and think about how I come up with my food, I wouldn't know how to explain it. It just comes to me. It's about textures and colors and contrasts." The results are an eclectic blend, as witnessed by the fusion of ingredients in Queen's rich and flavorful menu.

$\mathscr{S}$hrimp Bisque

Serves 6

STOCK

- ¼ cup canola oil
- 1-2 pounds shrimp, crab or lobster shells
- 2 large Spanish onions, peeled and chopped
- 4 carrots, peeled and chopped
- 1 teaspoon chopped garlic
- ½ teaspoon red pepper flakes
- 2 cups white wine
- 1 small can tomato paste
- 1 teaspoon dried thyme
- 1 teaspoon dried tarragon
- 4 bay leaves
- 5 peppercorns
- 4 quarts water

BISQUE

- 5 tablespoons butter
- ½ cup all-purpose flour
- 3⅓ cups shrimp stock
- 1 cup tomato puree (strained of seeds)
- 1 vanilla bean
- ⅔ cup heavy cream
- ½ cup dry sherry
- ⅓ cup veal demi-glace (or beef stock)
- 1 teaspoon lavender, finely chopped
- 1⅓ cups shiitake mushrooms, julienned
- 1 cup raw shrimp, shelled and chopped (¼ pound medium shrimp)
- Salt & freshly ground white pepper

To make stock: In a large stockpot, heat oil over medium-high heat. Add shells, stirring until lightly toasted. Add garlic and pepper flakes, and sauté until lightly toasted. Deglaze pan with white wine and add remaining stock ingredients. Cook until stock is reduced by half. Skim as necessary and strain.

To make bisque: In a large saucepan, melt butter over medium heat. Add flour and whisk until smooth. Cook until lightly toasted. Slowly whisk in shrimp stock to avoid lumps. Add tomato puree. Split vanilla bean and scrape inside of pod into soup. (Pod can be removed before serving.) Add cream, sherry, and demi-glace. Bring mixture to a boil and simmer for 10 minutes. Skim off any scum that accumulates on top of the soup. Add mushrooms, shrimp, and lavender. Cook an additional 2 minutes. Season with salt and pepper to taste.

The key to this rich and creamy soup is a flavorful shrimp or shellfish stock. Lobster, shrimp, crawfish, and crab shells in any combination can also be used.

Crispy Ravioli
with Caramelized Onion Vinaigrette

Serves 6

1½ cups mascarpone cheese
⅓ cup Parmesan cheese
⅓ cup Gorgonzola cheese
2 teaspoons canola oil
3 onions, julienned
2 teaspoons brown sugar
½ cup balsamic vinegar

⅓ cup olive oil
2 tablespoons chopped basil
6 slices apple-smoked bacon
6 pasta squares or egg-roll wrappers
2-3 heads frisée, cleaned
Salt & freshly ground black pepper

To make filling: In a meduim sized bowl, combine mascarpone, Parmesan, and Gorgonzola cheeses, season with salt and pepper, and chill.

To make vinaigrette: In a large skillet, heat canola oil over high heat. Add onions and sauté until translucent. Add brown sugar and deglaze with vinegar. Cook for 1 minute and remove from heat. In a large bowl, combine onion mixture with olive oil and basil. Season with salt and pepper to taste. Set aside.

Cook bacon until browned, but not too crispy. Keep warm.

To assemble: Lay out pasta squares or egg-roll wrappers. Moisten edges with a flour-water mixture. Place a dollop of the cheese mixture in the center, dividing equally among the 6 squares. Fold squares in half, forming a triangle; squeeze out air pockets. *(Raviolis may be made ahead and chilled until ready to cook.)*

Deep-fat fry the ravioli at 350° F for 30 seconds on each side. Keep flipping until lightly browned. Drain on paper towels.

On warm plates, spoon a portion of the vinaigrette on the front of each plate. Toss frisée with some of the vinaigrette. Place salad toward the back of the plate, and ravioli in front. Place cooked bacon on top of the ravioli and garnish with grated Parmesan cheese.

Ravioli assumes a new identity when it is deep-fried and accompanied by apple-smoked bacon and the rich flavor of caramelized onions.

Roasted Pork Loin
with Five-Spice Peach Glaze & Parsnip Puree

Serves 6

2 pounds parsnips
2 cups (4 sticks) butter
1-2 bunches watercress, cleaned, large
    stems removed
1 12-ounce bottle of stout or any
    strong-flavored beer
1 large egg
    Dash of chili oil
2½ cups cornstarch
2 pound center cut boneless pork loin

Sea salt
3 tablespoons minced fresh ginger
½ teaspoon minced garlic
3 tablespoons shallots, finely diced
1 cup chicken stock
1 cup veal demi-glace
4 peaches, peeled and cut into chunks
3 tablespoons honey mixed with 1½
    teaspoons five-spice powder

This satisfying pork dish mixes the sweetness of fresh peaches with pungent Chinese seasonings. It's one of my favorites.
∾

Preheat oven to 425° F.

To make parsnips: Peel parsnips, cut into chunks, and cover with cold water in a saucepan. Cook over medium heat until tender, drain well. Puree in food processor with 1 stick butter, salt, and white pepper. Keep warm.

To make tempura batter: In a bowl, mix beer, egg, chili oil, and cornstarch. Season with salt and pepper just before using, or batter will separate. Mix watercress in tempura batter. Drain well and drop watercress in batches into deep fat fryer for 10-20 seconds. Remove and drain well. *(May be prepared ahead of time and kept warm.)*

To prepare pork: Cut pork into

(continued on next page)

(Roasted Pork Loin continued)

two pieces, dust with five-spice powder, and season well with sea salt. Heat a thick, flat-bottomed pan with 1 gallon capacity over medium heat. When pan is hot, add the pork, fat side down, and sear on all sides.

Put pan in oven and cook for 15-25 minutes or until meat thermometer reads 140-160° F. Remove meat from oven and keep warm.

To make sauce: Using the same pan the pork was cooked in, add 3 sticks butter, ginger, garlic, shallots, honey/five-spice mixture, and peaches. Cook over high heat until bubbly. Add chicken stock, continue boiling until emulsified. Add veal stock, boiling until sauce is thickened, about 5 minutes. Season with salt and black and white pepper to taste.

To assemble: Slice pork loin into ¼-inch slices. On each plate, put a dollop of parsnip puree. Fan out the pork slices and glaze with the sauce. Top with fried watercress.

Apple, Celery Root & Endive Salad

Serves 6

VINAIGRETTE
- 1 tablespoon toasted sesame seeds
- ¼ cup rice wine vinegar
- 1 teaspoon chopped cilantro
- 2 tablespoons lime juice
- ½ teaspoon minced garlic
- ½ teaspoon minced orange peel
- 1 teaspoon ginger
  Salt & freshly ground black pepper
- 1 tablespoon sesame oil
- ¾ cup canola oil

SALAD
- 2 Granny Smith apples, skinned and julienned
- 2 heads endive, julienned
- ½ celery root, skinned and julienned
- 1 red pepper, julienned
- 1 bunch watercress, cleaned
- 1 cup basil leaves
- ½ cup cilantro leaves
- 6 radicchio leaves
  Wonton wrappers, finely julienned and deep-fried for garnish
- 2 tablespoons toasted sesame seeds for garnish

To make vinaigrette: In a stainless steel bowl, whisk together first 8 dressing ingredients. Whisk in sesame and canola oils until emulsified.

In a large bowl, toss apples, endive, celery root, pepper, watercress, basil, and cilantro with ¾ cup vinaigrette. On 6 chilled salad plates, place one radicchio leaf. Fill with salad mixture. Garnish with wonton strips and sesame seeds.

Pecan & Marzipan Gelato Cake

Serves 10

2 cups toasted pecans
2¾ cups heavy cream
1¼ cups milk
6 large eggs, separated

3 ounces marzipan or almond paste
2 cups sugar
1 cup water

In a food processor, grind 1 cup of pecans. Chop the other 1 cup and set both aside.

In a double boiler mix together ¾ cup cream, milk, and egg yolks. Cook, stirring until mixture coats the back of a spoon, about 10 minutes. Remove from heat. Add marzipan, and stir to incorporate. Set aside until cooled.

Meanwhile, in a small saucepan boil sugar and water until it reaches 150° F. In a large bowl, whip egg whites to soft peaks and slowly drizzle in sugar syrup while continuing to beat. Whip until

cooled, about 15 minutes. Fold in the cooled custard. Whip remaining 2 cups of cream to stiff peaks. Fold into custard/egg white mixture, along with ground pecans. Pour into a 10-inch springform pan, top with chopped pecans, and freeze at least 8 hours.

To unmold, wrap a hot towel around the outside of the mold before releasing the sides. Drizzle fruit puree or chocolate sauce onto each plate. Top with a wedge of cake on plate and drizzle again with sauce.

A frozen delight that makes a perfect ending to any meal. I like to serve it with a fruit puree or chocolate sauce.

e/b

Peggy Smith

Salute to Summer

❦

Corn Velouté
with
Tomato Concassé

———

Summer
Lobster Salad

———

Garden Salad
with
Roasted
Chanterelles
& Shallots

———

Fresh
Strawberries
with
Chez Panisse
Mascarpone

CHARDONNAY
Acacia
or
Argyle

SOON AFTER SHE MOVED to California in 1977, Peggy Smith set her sights on working at Chez Panisse. Smith would dutifully drop her résumé off at the restaurant once a month but received little encouragement. Soon after the upstairs cafe opened in 1980 she arrived for her monthly visit and this time was given an apron. Smith says she worked for quite a while before she knew she was officially hired. "I just kept coming back every day hoping that eventually I'd get a paycheck." She's been there ever since. As chef and manager of the cafe, Smith has been an integral part of the restaurant's enduring popularity. She offers a bird's-eye view of how things work at the upstairs of the remodeled home that houses the cafe at Chez Panisse in Berkeley.

"The cafe menu changes every day and usually includes seven or eight salads and four or five entrées, several pizzas from the woodburning oven, and seven or eight desserts," she says. Smith estimates that Chez Panisse gets 99 percent of its produce from within a fifty-mile radius of the restaurant.

There are twenty-one cooks in the bustling cafe that serves lunch and dinner to more than 400 people a day. In 1988 Alice Waters decided to try the concept of job sharing. There would be two chefs who would each cook three days a week and be responsible for managerial work the other two days. Smith and Catherine Brandel were appointed the first co-chefs. Very comfortable with the versatile nature of her job, Smith looks for ways to improve the working environment. In an effort to put the cooks' pay on a par with the waitstaff, the restaurant now adds a service charge to the check in lieu of tips.

The proceeds are divided by the cooks and waiters. Smith shows no signs of ever wanting to leave this utopian existence. "Our ingredients are the best, it's a beautiful part of the world, and people are paid a really decent wage to work here."

For this summer menu, Smith offers two of her favorite things—lobster and corn.

"I have a very hard time with really rich menus. This one sounds much richer than it is. The soup is made with a vegetable stock base, and the sauce for the lobster is a light and delicious reduction."

Garden Salad with Roasted Chanterelles & Shallots

Serves 4

3 cups chanterelle mushrooms, cleaned and quartered
4 shallots, peeled and cut in ¼-inch slices
½ cup extra virgin olive oil
2 sprigs fresh thyme leaves
1 clove fresh garlic, slivered

Salt & freshly ground black pepper
1 lemon, juiced
2 tablespoons sherry vinegar
1 tablespoon balsamic vinegar
Zest of ½ lemon
4 handfuls mixed garden lettuces, washed, dried and torn

To roast vegetables: Preheat oven to 300° F.

In a small roasting pan, toss mushrooms and shallots with ¼ cup of the olive oil. Add thyme, garlic, and salt and pepper to taste. Cover pan with foil and roast for 20 minutes. Remove foil and roast about 20 minutes more, until mushrooms and shallots are tender but still maintain some structure. Remove from oven. Let cool to room temperature. Just before serving, dress with lemon juice and salt and pepper to taste.

To make vinaigrette: In a small bowl, whisk sherry and balsamic vinegars into the remaining ¼ cup of the olive oil. Taste on lettuce just prior to serving to be sure the acid balance is correct. At the last minute add the lemon zest and salt and pepper to taste.

To serve: In a large bowl, toss lettuce with the vinaigrette. (When dressing, add half of the vinaigrette and toss lightly, add more dressing as needed, careful not to overdress or the flavors of the lettuce do not come through.) Mound one handful of salad in the center of 4 room-temperature salad plates. Distribute the roasted vegetables around the perimeter of the salad, and sprinkle a few on top.

This recipe works well with the summer chanterelle mushrooms, which are usually dry but still have a strong mushroom flavor. This salad may be served as a first course or after an entrée such as the lobster.

એ

Summer Lobster Salad

Serves 4

A perfect summer salad that incorporates many of the delicious ingredients the season has to offer. While the recipe requires attention, it is worth the effort.

∽

3 1¼-1½ pound lobsters
2 tablespoons plus ½ cup extra virgin olive oil
1 red bell pepper, seeded and coarsely chopped
2 carrots, peeled and coarsely chopped
1 medium yellow onion, coarsely chopped
1 tomato, seeded and coarsely chopped
1 bay leaf
   Shells from the cooked lobster
2 tablespoons cognac
1 cup chicken stock
½ cup cream

½ red onion, minced
2 shallots, peeled and minced
¼ cup champagne vinegar or Meyer lemon juice
   Salt & freshly ground black pepper
4 large handfuls (1½ pounds) mixed garden lettuces, washed, dried, and torn
½ pound small green beans, blanched
½ pound baby carrots, blanched
1 pound new potatoes, roasted with olive oil, garlic, and thyme
2 red bell peppers, roasted and peeled
½ pound cherry tomatoes, stemmed and halved

To cook lobster: In a large lobster pot, bring salted water to a boil. Add lobsters and cook 12 minutes for the 1¼ pound and 13 minutes for the 1½ pound. Remove from water and let cool. With a sharp knife, split each lobster in half lengthwise and detach the claws from the body. Extract the lobster meat from the tail, and clean the head cavity of any gills and gravel sacs. Next, crack the claws and extract the meat. Save the shells. Place lobster meat in a covered container and store in the refrigerator until ready to serve.

To make sauce: In a large stockpot, heat 2 tablespoons of olive oil over medium heat, add peppers, carrots, yellow onions, tomatoes, and bay leaf and sauté until the onions are translucent, about 5 minutes. Add lobster shells and continue to sauté, stirring continuously to keep the ingredients from sticking, for 4 minutes more. Deglaze the mixture with cognac and continue to cook for 1 minute more. Add

chicken stock and enough water to cover the ingredients. Reduce heat to low and simmer for 50 minutes. Strain the broth, discard the vegetables and shells, and return the broth to stove over low heat. Simmer until reduced by half. Add cream and again simmer the broth until reduced by half. Remove from the heat and let cool. Meanwhile, in a large bowl, place red onions, shallots, and vinegar or lemon juice.

Slowly whisk the cooled stock into the macerated shallots. Whisk the remaining ½ cup olive oil into mixture and add salt and pepper to taste.

To assemble: Slice the reserved lobster tail into ½-inch medallions. Cut claws in half lengthwise.

On each of 4 chilled plates place 3 lobster claw halves.

In a large bowl, toss greens lightly with some of the reserved sauce and arrange on a chilled plate. It is important to dress the greens separately to keep them from bruising. In the same bowl, dress the lobster in the sauce and distribute evenly on the salad greens, placing most of the lobster in the center of the plates, with the claws toward the outside of the plate. In the same large bowl, toss blanched green beans and carrots, roasted potatoes and peppers, and cherry tomatoes with the sauce and distribute evenly on the plates. Serve immediately.

Corn Velouté with Tomato Concassé

Serves 4

4   medium tomatoes of various colors
3½ cups fresh sweet corn, about 4 ears, removed from the cob (reserve the cobs for stock)
1   handful fresh basil, cut into thin strips, reserve the stems for stock
1   bay leaf

2   tablespoons unsalted butter
1   tablespoon extra virgin olive oil
2   large onions, diced
2   egg yolks
1   cup cream
    Salt & freshly ground black pepper

This recipe was developed to highlight the sweet flavor of freshly picked corn, enriching it with a little egg and cream to add depth. It's perfect for a summer lunch with a salad on the side.

To make tomato concassé: Use a sharp knife to score the bottom of each tomato with a small cross. Blanch tomatoes in simmering water for about 10 seconds. Remove the tomatoes from water and plunge into ice water to cool quickly.

Peel the tomatoes carefully, making sure not to bruise the meat. Cut the tomatoes in half (around their equator, not through the stem end). Carefully extract the seeds and jelly. Reserve the juice from the seeds to use later.

Dice tomato meat and hold in the reserved juice. Concassé may be stored, covered in refrigerator, but should be drained and brought to room temperature before adding to soup.

To make stock: In a large stockpot over medium heat, bring to a simmer 4 cups of water, the reserved 4 corncobs and basil stems, and a bay leaf. Cook for about 20 minutes. Strain the liquid and discard the cobs and herbs.

To make soup: In a large heavy-bottomed pot, lightly heat butter and olive oil over low heat. Add onions and cook until translucent and soft, about 5-10 minutes. Add 4 cups of the reserved stock, bring to a simmer and cook for 5 minutes. Add corn and cook for 3 minutes more. Remove from heat.

Puree the soup in a blender, then pass through a strainer to eliminate the skin from the corn kernels. *(The recipe can be made ahead to this point and continued just before serving.)*

To finish the velouté, return the corn soup base to the cleaned stockpot and bring to a simmer over low heat.

In a small bowl, whisk the cream and egg yolks together. Slowly ladle ½ cup of the soup base into the cream/egg mixture. (If cream and egg mixture is added directly to the soup base, it will curdle.) Add the cream mixture to the soup base. Season with salt and pepper to taste.

Garnish with the reserved tomato concassé and the basil chiffonade and serve immediately.

Fresh Strawberries
with Chez Panisse Mascarpone

Serves 4

1 **quart cream**
¼ **teaspoon tartaric acid***

2 **pints fresh strawberries**

In a double boiler heat cream to 180° F.
Stir in the tartaric acid, stir for 30
seconds and remove from heat. Stir for
2 minutes more after removing from heat.
Pour into a stainless steel container and
cover lightly. Refrigerate for 12 hours
before serving.

Cut strawberries in half lengthwise.
Arrange on 4 plates with a dollop of
mascarpone.

**Note: Tartaric acid (not cream of tartar)
is an ingredient that can be found at stores that
sell beer or wine-making ingredients. If unable
to find tartaric acid, combine 8 ounces
mascarpone cheese with ¼ cup whipping cream
and mix together until a creamy consistency.*

*Fresh strawberries
with creamy
mascarpone cheese
is a perfectly simple
delicious dessert.
The mascarpone can
be used with
different fruits, such
as fresh dates or
poached pears. At
Chez Panisse we
make our own
mascarpone.*

෫ා

Johanne Killeen

IT WAS AN EXPENSIVE CAMERA that set in motion a chain of events that would propel Johanne Killeen into the restaurant business. She was trying to support herself as a freelance photographer in the early '70s, when she was approached by a friend who asked her to help with a food concession at Brown University. Having just spent far too much money on a camera, she agreed. In 1975, this same friend started a restaurant in Providence, Rhode Island. He invited Killeen to be his pastry chef, and George Germon, a freelance architect, to be the chef.

This unlikely professional pairing eventually led Killeen and Germon to love, marriage, and the start of a business that would bring in a steady income. "Our original concept was to sell pizza by the pound—an idea we saw in the Jewish ghetto of Rome. They put out big trays of pizza with great toppings—things that were very unusual to us: artichoke bottoms, sliced potatoes and rosemary, no tomatoes," recalls Killeen. "Two days before we opened, George said to me, 'I don't want to be a pizza maker.' So we changed the whole concept of the restaurant in two days! We opened with baked pasta and vegetables that you might find on an antipasto table, and we made little pissaladières (flaky, pizzalike tarts). As soon as we opened the doors, we realized, this is it, we both really loved it."

Killeen and Germon's is a partnership that has become well-known in the food world. Their restaurant, Al Forno, which opened in 1980, was one of the first restaurants dedicated to the rustic regional Italian cuisine that has since become a passion for American restaurant-goers. "We talk about our memories of the food of Italy, not to try to reproduce it, but to learn from the flavors and the tastes," says Killeen. "The Italians do as little as possible to food—just try to get the inherent goodness out of the ingredients, not masking one ingredient with another, but allowing each to live on its own. We have adopted this philosophy in our cooking."

Killeen says that early on they became disciplined in working with simple ingredients and finding the best of what was available. This proved quite a challenge in the early '80s in Providence. "I'm sure we're responsible for bringing in a lot of new products to this city—nothing fancy, because that's not really part of our cooking—but I actually think we brought romaine lettuce here!"

This meal offers a lovely combination of textures and flavors, with dishes inspired by everything from a special local turnip to a tradition of the Tuscan harvest to Killeen's childhood baking efforts.

Turnip Cream Soup

Serves 8

¼ cup (½ stick) unsalted butter
2 large onions, peeled and thinly sliced
1 large Westport turnip or yellow rutabaga, peeled and diced

7½ cups water
2 teaspoons kosher salt
6-8 Empire apples
2 cups heavy cream

In a stockpot, melt butter over low heat. Add onions and cook, covered, until very soft, 15-20 minutes.

Add turnips or rutabagas, 6 cups of water, and salt. Raise the heat, bring to a boil, then reduce the heat to low. Simmer, covered, until the turnips are very soft and break up easily when pressed with the back of a spoon, about 1 hour.

Meanwhile, core and quarter apples, leaving the skins on. Cut each quarter in half horizontally.

In a small saucepan, combine the apples and 1½ cups of water. Bring to a boil and cook, uncovered, until the apples disintegrate. Raise the heat and cook until the water has evaporated; as the liquid reduces, the sugars will concentrate. Keep a close watch, stirring constantly to avoid scorching.

In a blender, puree the apples and set aside. You should have about 2 cups of puree.

Puree the turnips with their liquid and return the puree to a clean pot. Over low heat, add cream. Bring to a boil, stirring constantly.

Ladle the soup into heated bowls and garnish by swirling the apple puree in the center.

In the Rhode Island area we have a wonderful vegetable called the Westport turnip. This turnip is fairly sweet to begin with and the addition of apple puree brings it to another level.

Mushroom Salad with Shaved Parmigiano

Serves 4-6

12 ounces fresh white mushrooms
¼ teaspoon kosher salt
½-1 teaspoon fresh thyme leaves
    or 24-30 fresh Italian parsley leaves
1 4-6 ounce piece Parmigiano-Reggiano cheese
2 lemons
6-9 tablespoons extra virgin olive oil
    Freshly ground black pepper

Wipe mushrooms to remove any dirt clinging to them, trim the stem ends, and cut vertically into paper-thin slices.

Divide half the mushrooms among 4-6 individual salad bowls, sprinkle each with a pinch of salt and thyme or parsley.

With a vegetable peeler, shave a layer of Parmigiano-Reggiano over the mushrooms. Repeat with the remaining mushrooms, salt, and cheese.

Cut 1 lemon into 4-6 wedges for garnish. Squeeze the juice of the other lemon into a small bowl. Set aside.

Drizzle 1-1½ tablespoons of olive oil over each salad, pour on the lemon juice, sprinkle with pepper to taste. Garnish with lemon wedges.

Spaghettini with Spicy Lentil Sauce

Serves 6-8

4 tablespoons olive oil
½ cup (1 stick) unsalted butter
1 cup chopped fresh fennel
2 carrots, peeled and chopped
2 large onions, peeled and chopped
1 tablespoon minced fresh garlic
1 teaspoon kosher salt
½ teaspoon crushed red pepper flakes
1 teaspoon Hungarian sweet paprika
1 teaspoon Hungarian hot paprika
8 ounces lentils
5 cups water
1½ pounds imported spaghettini or linguine fini

In a large saucepan, heat olive oil and 2 tablespoons of the butter. Add fennel, carrots, onions, garlic, salt, and red pepper. Sauté until the vegetables are soft, 15-20 minutes. Add both paprikas and sauté for 2 minutes more to coat the vegetables. Add lentils and water. Bring to a boil, lower the heat, and simmer until the lentils are soft, but not falling apart, about 18-22 minutes.

In a large stockpot, bring 5 quarts of salted water to a boil, drop in the pasta, and boil it until still quite firm, 4-5 minutes.

Drain the pasta and add it to the lentil sauce with the remaining butter. Toss for 1-2 minutes until the pasta is al dente. Serve immediately.

Roasted Sausages & Grapes

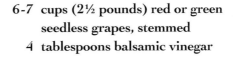

Serves 6 to 8

1½ pounds hot Italian sausage	6-7 cups (2½ pounds) red or green
1½ pounds sweet Italian sausage	seedless grapes, stemmed
3 tablespoons unsalted butter	4 tablespoons balsamic vinegar

Preheat oven to 500° F. In a large pan, cover sausages with water and parboil for 8 minutes to rid them of excess fat.

Melt butter in large flameproof roasting pan. Add grapes and toss to coat. With tongs, transfer the sausages to the roasting pan and push them down into the grapes so the sausages don't brown too quickly. Roast in the oven, turning the sausages once, for 20-25 minutes or until the grapes are soft and the sausages have browned. With a slotted spoon, transfer the sausages and grapes to a heated serving platter. Place the roasting pan on the stovetop over medium-high heat. Add balsamic vinegar, scraping up any browned bits on the bottom of the roasting pan. Allow the vinegar and juices to reduce until they are thick and syrupy.

Pour the sauce over the sausages and grapes and serve immediately, accompanied by Al Forno's Mashed Potatoes (page 122).

This Tuscan-inspired dish is very popular at the time of the grape harvest, when Italians use grapes right from the vineyard. It has a nice balance of ingredients: the richness of the sausages and the sweetness of the grapes are pulled together by the balsamic vinegar.

❧

 Al Forno's Mashed Potatoes

Serves 6

2 pounds small red potatoes, quartered, skins on

½ cup heavy cream

½ cup (1 stick) unsalted butter, room temperature

1 teaspoon kosher salt or to taste

In a large saucepan, cover potatoes with 1 inch of water. Bring to a boil, lower heat, and simmer until the potatoes are soft, about 15 minutes.

Drain and return the potatoes to the saucepan. Over very low heat, coarsely mash the potatoes with an old-fashioned masher or two large forks, gradually adding cream and butter. Stir in salt.

 Apple-Crisp Crostata

Serves 6-8

DOUGH

1 cup (2 sticks) very cold unsalted butter

2 cups unbleached all-purpose flour

¼ cup superfine sugar

½ teaspoon kosher salt

¼ cup ice water

CROSTATA

10 ounces dough

¼ cup unbleached all-purpose flour

¼ cup superfine sugar

¼ cup (½ stick) cold unsalted butter

1½ pounds (about 3 large) Macintosh, Macoun, or Empire apples

To make dough: Cut butter into ½-inch cubes. Since it softens rapidly with handling, return the cubes to the refrigerator for at least 10 minutes while setting up the food processor and gathering the dry ingredients.

Place flour, sugar, and salt in the bowl of a food processor fitted with the steel blade. Pulse a few times to combine.

Add the butter, first tossing the cubes quickly with your fingers to coat each cube with flour, taking care not to touch the blade. (This prevents the butter cubes from adhering and helps them break apart and combine more evenly with the flour.) Pulse 15 times, or until the butter particles are the size of small peas.

With the motor running, add ice water all at once through the feed tube. Process for about 10 seconds, stopping the machine before the dough becomes a solid mass.

Cover the dough completely with aluminum foil and refrigerate for at least 1 hour.

Note: This recipes makes 18-20 ounces of dough. I like to keep the extra in my freezer for unexpected gatherings or last-minute desserts. The dough may be refrigerated up to 2 days or frozen for up to 2 weeks.

To make crostata: Preheat oven to 450° F.

On a lightly floured surface roll 10 ounces of tart dough into an 11-inch circle. Transfer it to a baking sheet.

Combine flour and sugar in a small mixing bowl. With two knives, or with your fingertips, blend in butter until the mixture crumbles and holds together in irregular lumps. Set aside.

Peel, core, and quarter apples. Cut each quarter into 3 chunks. Cover the tart dough with the apple chunks, leaving a 1½-inch border around the outside edge.

Cover the apples with the butter mixture. Raise the dough border to enclose the sides of the tart, letting it drape gently over the fruit. Press down on the dough at the baking sheet, snugly securing the sides and the bottom; be careful not to mash the fruit. Gently pinch the soft pleats that form from the draping.

Bake the tart for about 20 minutes, until the crust is golden and the apples are soft. Check the tart after 12 minutes; if the topping is browning too quickly, place a sheet of foil loosely over the top for the remainder of the baking time.

Cool the tart on a rack for about 10 minutes and serve warm.

Joyce Goldstein

JOYCE GOLDSTEIN'S CHILDHOOD home in Brooklyn was not a culinary haven, but she loved the family excursions to restaurants in New York. There she learned her first lessons about good food and good service—the hallmarks of her craft today as chef and owner of the acclaimed Square One Restaurant in San Francisco.

Her interest in all things Mediterranean stems from a year and a half spent in Italy starting in 1959, when her former husband was a Fulbright Scholar in architecture. They had no refrigerator, but lived across from a huge open market, so Goldstein marketed daily. As the couple traveled extensively through the area, Goldstein learned everything she could about what they were eating, and she made mental notes of tastes she liked and wanted to be able to create again on her own.

As an artist in the early '60s, Goldstein exhibited her paintings at the San Francisco Museum of Art and other venues. But the arrival of three children in quick succession made her turn her artistic energies from painting to cooking. It was much easier to be creative cooking than to find significant time to work in the studio, she says. "I would read cookbooks at night in bed, and research and market and then cook and cook."

Eventually Goldstein began to give private cooking lessons and teach classes, and in 1971 she founded the California Street Cooking School. Goldstein never intended to enter the restaurant business. In 1981, as a favor to Alice Waters, she filled in at Chez Panisse. She found that not only did she prefer working in a restaurant to teaching, she had a real flair for it. Within a year she was chef and manager of the cafe at Chez Panisse. She stayed for three years before she decided she wanted the autonomy of her own restaurant.

In 1984 she opened Square One, featuring classic dishes from around the world, although Mediterranean food is her primary passion. She describes her food as "tasty, no bullshit, big flavors, as authentic to the spirit of the country as possible, using good ingredients and some finesse." Goldstein's inspiration for her dishes comes from her library of 3,000 cookbooks, from travel and from tasting. "Many things are new to the American public that people think we are making up, but these dishes have actually been around for hundreds of years." She tries to find dishes from different cultures that she thinks Americans are finally ready to eat. In this pursuit, as in all others—artist, teacher, chef, writer, culinary scholar, and community activist—she has been enormously successful. The sustained popularity of her restaurant and her award-winning cookbooks attest to the fact that Americans are indeed ready to try the foods of different cultures, especially when presented by this talented artist.

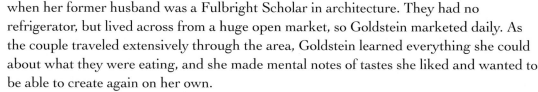

A Tempting Mediterranean Menu

☙

Asparagus with
Mint Vinaigrette
& Almonds

Turkish
Red Lentil Soup

Leg of Lamb
with Mint & Garlic

Carrots & Fennel
with Dill

Roasted Pepper &
Celery Salad
with
Tomato Vinaigrette

Baked Figs

CABERNET SAUVIGNON
Laurel Glen
or
Spotteswoode

Asparagus with Mint Vinaigrette & Almonds

Serves 6

1½ pounds asparagus, trimmed and
    peeled if necessary
¼ cup plus 2 tablespoons fresh lemon
    juice
¾ cup chopped fresh mint
1¼ cups mild olive oil

¼ cup sherry vinegar
1 teaspoon sugar
½ teaspoon salt
½ cup almonds, chopped coarsely and
    toasted

In a large pot of boiling water, cook asparagus until tender crisp. Refresh under cold water, drain, and pat dry. Set aside.

To make vinaigrette: Combine ¼ cup lemon juice and ¼ cup mint in a small saucepan. Bring to a boil over high heat; remove from heat. Steep for 10 minutes. Strain into a mixing bowl, reserving liquid. There should be ¼ cup of mint infusion. To the mint infusion add the remaining ½ cup of mint, 2 tablespoons lemon juice, olive oil, vinegar, sugar, and salt, and whisk together.

Distribute the reserved asparagus on 6 salad plates. Drizzle with the vinaigrette. Sprinkle with chopped almonds.

When asparagus is in season, you'll want to make this refreshing first course. The asparagus can be blanched ahead of time and dressed at the last minute. You can also serve this vinaigrette on cooked leeks, beets, and artichokes.

Turkish Red Lentil Soup

Serves 6

There are many variations on Turkish red lentil soup. Some add a little chopped carrot to the onions, some omit the milk, and some make this with green lentils. Garnishes range from simple croutons to mint and croutons, to mint and yogurt, to melted butter with paprika and mint.

3 tablespoons unsalted butter	1 cup milk (optional); if no milk, add fresh lemon juice to taste
1½ cups chopped onions	Salt & freshly ground black pepper
1 carrot, chopped (optional)	Ground red pepper to taste
1 cup red lentils, washed and drained	2 slices bread, about ½ inch thick, crusts removed
1½ teaspoons paprika	3 tablespoons chopped fresh mint or 1 tablespoon crumbled dried mint
2 tablespoons tomato paste (optional)	
6 cups chicken stock or water	

In a medium saucepan, melt butter over moderate heat. Add onions, lentils, and carrots. Cook, stirring occasionally, about 5 minutes. Add paprika and tomato paste and stir well to mix. Reduce heat to low and cook for a few minutes. Gradually add stock or water, stirring constantly. Simmer, uncovered, until lentils are very soft, about 30 minutes.

Transfer to blender or food processor and puree until smooth. Return to saucepan and add milk or lemon juice, salt, pepper, and red pepper. Simmer over low heat until heated through.

Toast bread until crisp and golden on both sides, then cut into cubes. Or, first cut bread into cubes and then sauté in butter until golden.

Ladle into individual bowls. Sprinkle with mint and croutons.

Leg of Lamb with Mint & Garlic

Serves 6-8

¾ cup chopped fresh mint

2 tablespoons finely minced garlic

¼ cup finely minced bacon or pancetta

1 tablespoon paprika

1 teaspoon salt, plus more to taste

½ teaspoon freshly ground black pepper, plus more to taste

2 tablespoons red wine vinegar

6 pound leg of lamb, boned and trimmed of fell and excess fat inside and out

¼ cup olive oil, mixed with 1 tablespoon red wine vinegar

In a small dish, combine mint, garlic, bacon, paprika, salt, pepper, and vinegar into a paste. Rub this mixture all over the inside of the lamb. Roll and tie lamb with white kitchen string. Wrap in plastic wrap and refrigerate for 12-24 hours.

Preheat oven to 400° F. Bring meat to room temperature. Put lamb on a rack in a roasting pan and brush lightly with olive oil mixture. Sprinkle lightly with salt and pepper. Roast for 45 minutes, basting with the remaining oil mixture, until thermometer reads 120° F for rare or 135-140° F for medium doneness. Remove from the oven. Let the lamb rest for 10 minutes, then slice. Serve with roasted potatoes.

While you could use this Spanish mint marinade on a boneless, butterflied leg of lamb and broil it, traditionally the boneless lamb is rubbed with the herb paste, rolled and tied, then roasted.

Carrots & Fennel with Dill

Serves 6

Cooked carrots are reliable and comforting but can be a little boring. Here's a way to add excitement to this sweet and tender root vegetable.

¼ cup olive oil
1 cup chopped onions
1 teaspoon toasted cumin seeds, ground
1 tablespoon sugar or honey
1½ pounds carrots, peeled and sliced ¼-inch thick (or cut into julienne strips on a mandoline)

Chicken stock or water as needed to cover
2 small bulbs fennel, trimmed, cored, and sliced thin
1 cup blanched fresh fava beans, peeled (optional)
Salt & freshly ground black pepper
4 tablespoons chopped fresh dill

In a large saucepan, heat olive oil over medium heat. Add onions and cook until tender and translucent, 8-10 minutes. Add cumin and sugar or honey and cook for 2 minutes longer. Add carrots and enough stock or water to just barely cover the carrots. Simmer covered, stirring from time to time until carrots are half cooked, about 10 minutes. Add fennel and continue to cook until the vegetables are tender and liquid is reduced, 8-10 minutes longer. During the last 3-5 minutes, add favas, if using.

Season with salt and pepper to taste. Sprinkle with chopped dill.

Roasted Pepper & Celery Salad with Tomato Vinaigrette

Serves 6

A colorful Mediterranean salad. The crunch of celery or fennel adds a nice texture.

1 cup mild olive oil
½ cup diced plum tomatoes
2 tablespoons tomato puree
¼ cup sherry vinegar
¼ cup raisins or currants, soaked in hot water until plump, drained
Salt & freshly ground black pepper

3 large red bell peppers, roasted, cut into ½-inch-wide strips
6 ribs celery, strings removed, sliced thinly on the diagonal or 2 large bulbs fennel, cut in half, cored, and thinly sliced

In a medium-sized bowl, whisk together olive oil, tomatoes, tomato puree, vinegar, raisins or currants, salt and pepper to taste. Adjust sweet and sour ratio to taste. If too tart add a pinch of sugar.

Add peppers and celery or fennel, and toss.

Baked Figs

Serves 6

24 small, ripe, black Mission or
    Adriatic figs, or 12 large figs
⅓ cup honey
½ cup fresh orange juice
¼ cup brandy or Grand Marnier
3-4 small bay leaves

A few thin strips orange zest
½ cup toasted chopped hazelnuts
    (optional)
    Crème fraîche, mascarpone, or thick
    sweetened yogurt

Preheat oven to 350° F.

Prick figs in a few places with the tines of a fork so that they may absorb the cooking juices. Place in a baking dish. Combine the honey, orange juice, and brandy or Grand Marnier, and pour over the figs. Add a little water, if necessary, so that the liquid covers the bottom of the dish by about ¼ inch. Tuck in bay leaves and zest.

Cover and bake for 25-35 minutes, basting occasionally. Sprinkle with chopped hazelnuts, crème fraîche, mascarpone or thick sweetened yogurt, if using.

Note: Substitute lemon zest and lemon juice instead of orange if desired. In Spain they use anisette instead of brandy.

These are a light and fragrant ending to a rich meal. You may serve the figs plain or topped with a dollop of sweetened thick yogurt, crème fraîche, or mascarpone.

Nancy Flume

Seattle Seafood Sublime

∽

Paragon
Curried Mussels

———

Belgian Endive Spears
with Shrimp
&
Walnut-Raspberry
Dressing

———

Spicy Cajun Prawns

———

Grissini

———

Almond Tuiles

SAUVIGNON BLANC
SÉMILLON BLEND
Matanzas Creek
or
Merryvale

AS A STUDENT at the University of Washington, Nancy Flume worked part-time as a waitress. She decided it might be more fun on the other side of the kitchen door, so she left college and enrolled in cooking school. Upon graduation in 1982 she jotted down a list of her favorite Seattle restaurants and proceeded to knock on their doors in search of a job. Her second stop was Adriatica, a small boutique restaurant serving Mediterranean food. The prep cook told her he was glad she'd appeared—he was planning to quit his job the following week but hadn't told the chef yet. Flume downed a drink for courage, cornered the chef, broke it to him that his prep cook was leaving, and informed him that she would be an able replacement. She got the job and stayed for thirteen years.

Clearly Flume had a natural affinity for the restaurant world. After doing prep work for three months, she was moved to the pantry; six months after that she found herself assisting the chef. She took over the kitchen in 1984. "I was very ambitious then, and they just kept moving me up. At the time it was terrifying," she recalls. During Flume's tenure, her cooking earned Adriatica many local and regional awards.

Her new restaurant, Paragon, opened in 1995. This neighborhood bistro in Seattle also has a lively bar and music scene—a change from the more formal atmosphere Flume was accustomed to. She describes Paragon's eclectic menu as American bistro fare. Although Flume includes satays, spring rolls, and quesadillas on her menu, her penchant is for the rustic Italian carpaccios, risottos, and pastas the restaurant features.

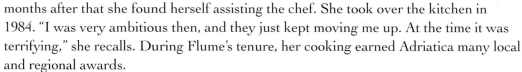

This menu celebrates Seattle's bountiful seafood and Flume's subtle touch with assertive ingredients. The simplicity of preparation will be a joy to the home cook. "I'm not one of those cooks who gets into food design and intricate plates," she says. "I think that's fine, but for me food is food. It should look great, but it doesn't have to become art. People should be entertained by food, but they shouldn't be overwhelmed by it."

Paragon Curried Mussels

Serves 4

3 tablespoons unsalted butter
½ large onion, chopped
2 teaspoons minced garlic
½ teaspoon ground cumin
½ teaspoon crushed red chilies
½ teaspoon turmeric
Pinch of ground cloves
½ teaspoon freshly ground black pepper

¼ teaspoon salt
2 tomatoes, peeled, cored, seeded, and chopped
2 pounds mussels, debearded
1 cup coconut milk
¼ cup fresh lemon juice
1 bunch cilantro, chopped

In a large, heavy skillet, melt butter over medium heat. Add onions and garlic and sauté until golden, about 5 minutes. Add cumin, chilies, turmeric, cloves, pepper, and salt; cook until aromatic, 2-3 minutes.

Add tomatoes, mussels, coconut milk, and lemon juice. Mix well; cover and simmer until mussels are all open, about 2-3 minutes. Remove and discard any mussels that have not opened.

Stir in cilantro, mix well, and serve immediately.

This colorful dish is great as a first course and is also wonderful with basmati rice as a main course. Serve with grilled pita bread and soup spoons to get every drop of sauce. I use mussels from Penn Cove on Whidbey Island, Washington, but any type will work.

Spicy Cajun Prawns

Serves 4

This piquant dish is a breeze to make. Adjust the cayenne to make it more or less spicy. It may be served over pasta or rice, and also works well as a first course.

⌒

½ cup (1 stick) unsalted butter
½ cup minced scallions
2 teaspoons minced garlic
¾ teaspoon salt
¼ teaspoon dried thyme leaves
½ teaspoon cayenne pepper
¼ teaspoon freshly ground white pepper
¼ teaspoon freshly ground black pepper

½ teaspoon ground cumin
½ pound quartered crimini mushrooms
½ cup julienned red bell pepper
1 pound prawns, shells removed, deveined
¼ cup shrimp stock, white wine, or clam juice
2 tablespoons fresh lemon juice
¼ cup chopped parsley

In a large sauté pan, melt ¼ cup butter over medium-high heat. Mix in scallions, garlic, and all the spices. Add mushrooms and red peppers; sauté for about 2 minutes. Add prawns, stock, wine or clam juice, and lemon juice. Bring to a simmer. Add the remaining ¼ cup of butter in small bits, swirling pan with each addition. When sauce thickens and prawns are just cooked, about 2 minutes, add parsley and serve immediately.

Grissini

Serves 4

The recipe for these crisp bread sticks originated in Turin, Italy. They are fun to eat and a good accompaniment to any salad or soup. Double the recipe to have extras on hand.

⌒

1 package active dry yeast
¾ cup warm water
2 cups all-purpose flour
1 teaspoon salt

1 teaspoon dried rosemary
2 teaspoons minced garlic
1 teaspoon coarsely ground black pepper

In a large bowl, mix yeast and water until softened. Add flour, salt, rosemary, garlic, and pepper, and stir until evenly mixed. Don't knead. Pat into a ball, cover, and let rise until doubled.

Preheat oven to 325° F. Roll dough onto floured board into a ¼-inch-thick rectangle. Cut into long ¼-inch-strips. Place on parchment on a baking sheet. Bake about 30 minutes, or until golden.

Belgian Endive Spears
with Shrimp & Walnut-Raspberry Dressing

Serves 4

DRESSING

1 large egg
1 tablespoon minced shallots
1 tablespoon Dijon mustard
½ teaspoon freshly ground black pepper
½ teaspoon salt
1 cup walnut oil
⅓ cup raspberry vinegar
½ cup heavy cream

SALAD

2 heads Belgian endive, washed and dried
½ pound best quality cooked shrimp meat, such as Chilean
4 ounces walnuts, toasted
4 ounces Roquefort cheese, crumbled
1 bunch watercress, stemmed, washed, and dried

To make dressing: In a food processor, blend egg, shallots, mustard, pepper, and salt. Gradually drizzle in oil, vinegar, and cream while running the processor. Chill.

Chill a large serving plate. Arrange 5 or 6 spears of endive in a sunburst pattern on the plate. Sprinkle shrimp over endive, drizzle dressing over, sprinkle with walnuts and cheese, arrange watercress in the center.

This elegant composed salad also tastes great when hearts of Bibb lettuce are substituted for the endive and all the ingredients are tossed together for a less formal presentation.

Almond Tuiles

Makes 1 dozen

1 cup whole almonds
3 tablespoons all-purpose flour
1 cup sugar
¼ cup (½ stick) unsalted butter

3 tablespoons milk
1 teaspoon pure vanilla extract
  Vanilla ice cream

In a food processor, combine almonds, flour, and sugar, pulsing just until coarsely chopped. Gradually add butter and pulse until barely combined. Scrape into a small mixing bowl; fold in milk and vanilla.

Chill well before using. *(You may store the dough tightly wrapped for several days or you can freeze it.)*

Preheat oven to 350° F. Place balls of dough, about the size of golf balls, 3 inches apart on a nonstick baking sheet. Bake 10-12 minutes or until golden brown. Let tuiles rest on sheet until cool enough to handle but still pliable, about 3 minutes. Mold each tuile over an inverted cup or small bowl to form into a "cup" shape. Let cool until set.

Fill each tuile with one scoop of vanilla ice cream or desired filling just before serving.

Note: Tuiles will keep well in an airtight container until ready to serve. However, they are quite fragile and should be stored where they will be undisturbed.

These crisp cookies are simple to make but dramatic on the plate. Tuiles can be shaped into a bowl, a tube, a "taco" shape, or even left flat. Here we fill them with ice cream, but tuiles offer delicious possibilities with mousse, berries, anything you like.

Anne Rosenzweig

AS WITH MANY OF HER COLLEAGUES, cooking was not Anne Rosenzweig's first career choice. She was trained as an anthropologist, and did field work in Africa, Nepal, and India, where she learned about a variety of indigenous cuisines. "Everywhere I lived people taught me how to cook as a way of introducing me to their community. Most of the countries were poor and had very few ingredients to cook with, but the food was always incredibly delicious to me. It's easy to make foie gras taste good, but if you can take simple ingredients like lentils and make them taste wonderful—that is something special."

Rosenzweig had always found the idea of cooking very intriguing, but didn't want to leave the field of anthropology. In the late '70s, though, she decided to take a job in a restaurant kitchen to satisfy her curiosity. She found an apprenticeship and, after her first day, was in love with the work. Following the European model, she worked twelve hours a day for free, for almost a year, working through each of the stations at the restaurant and voraciously reading cookbooks. She recalls the hazing process that the new recruit was subjected to: "I got to do all the stuff the chefs wouldn't do— like carrying an eighty-pound stockpot by myself. It was always 'more, more, faster, faster.' "

Today the native New Yorker presides over two popular Manhattan restaurants, Arcadia and The Lobster Club. Rosenzweig's approach to food is that "the taste is absolutely paramount. My job as chef is to really help bring out the essence of the food." At both of her restaurants she says there's a certain amount of whimsy in the menu, but Arcadia is meant to be an elegant, sophisticated restaurant, while The Lobster Club is more casual and allows her the freedom to do the "homey, earthy things" she can't do at Arcadia. At The Lobster Club there is a Mom's Meat Loaf and a Fish and Chips dish that change every day, while at Arcadia, Smoked Lobster with Celery Root Cakes and Tarragon Butter is the quintessential dish.

The recipes in this meal draw from both sources—from elegant hand-folded ravioli, to aromatic roasted chicken, to a dessert that takes shortcake to a new level.

$\mathscr{S}$weet Potato Ravioli
with Portobello Mushrooms & Apples

Serves 6

FILLING

- 1½ tablespoons olive oil
- ½ large onion, diced
- 5 cloves garlic, roughly chopped
- 2 tablespoons fresh sage, chopped
- 1½ large sweet potatoes, roasted and peeled
- ¼ cup toasted pine nuts
- ½ cup grated Parmesan cheese

RAVIOLI

- ½ large sweet potato, roasted and peeled
- 2 large eggs
- 2 tablespoons olive oil
- 2½-3 cups all-purpose flour
  Salt & freshly ground black pepper

GARNISH

- 4 tablespoons olive oil
- 2 large portobello mushrooms, diced
- 1 green apple, peeled, cored, and diced
- 1 large sweet potato, peeled, diced, and blanched
- ¼ cup chopped parsley
  Salt & freshly ground black pepper
  Crème fraîche

Here's a rich and colorful beginning to any meal. The delicate hand-folded ravioli has a creamy, pungent filling and is topped with a hearty garnish.

To make filling: In a large sauté pan, heat oil over medium heat. Add onions and garlic and sauté, stirring occasionally. Fold in chopped sage and cook for approximately one more minute. Transfer mixture to a food processor.

Chop sweet potato roughly. Place in food processor. Add pine nuts and cheese. Process all ingredients until smooth.

To make ravioli: In a food processor, combine sweet potato, eggs, and oil. Process until smooth. Add flour and continue to process until a stiff dough forms. Season with salt and pepper to taste. Put dough through a pasta machine until very thin. Cut into 4 x 4-inch squares.

To make garnish: In a large sauté pan, heat oil over medium heat. Add

(continued on next page)

(Sweet Potato Ravioli continued)

mushrooms and sauté until slightly crispy. Stir in apple and sweet potato. When vegetables are tender, but still crispy, about 5 minutes, fold in parsley. Season with salt and pepper to taste.

To assemble: In a small saucepan, heat filling.

In a large pot of boiling water, blanch pasta squares until just pliable. Drain pasta.

Lay two pasta squares on each plate. Place a spoonful of filling on bottom third of each pasta square. Fold square over to create triangle. Spoon garnish over and around pasta. Top with a dollop of crème fraîche.

Spitfire Sugar Cane Chicken with Hominy Cakes & Tomato-Papaya Salad

Serves 6

The sweet, aromatic marinade intensifies the flavor of chicken roasted with sugar cane and complemented by a tart fruit salad.

CHICKEN

- 3 2½ pound chickens, split and boned
- 1 tablespoon whole cumin
- 2 tablespoons coriander
- ½ teaspoon cardamom
- ¾ cup olive oil
- ¾ cup honey
- ¼ cup amber rock sugar (optional)
- 1 8-inch piece sugar cane

SALAD

- 6 plum tomatoes, peeled and seeded
- 1 medium papaya, peeled and seeded
- 2 kiwis, peeled
- 3 scallions, minced

- ½ cup olive oil
- ¼ cup fresh lemon juice
  Salt & freshly ground black pepper
- 1 cup baby greens

HOMINY CAKES

- ¾ cup all-purpose flour
- ½ cup plus 2 tablespoons grits
- ½ teaspoon salt
- 3 large eggs
- ¾ cup whole milk
- ½ cup plus 2 tablespoons water
- 3 tablespoons sweet butter, melted
- 2 tablespoons vegetable oil

To marinate chicken: Flatten chickens slightly with a mallet.

In a small skillet, toast whole cumin and coriander seeds until lightly smoking. Let cool. Grind finely. Combine with ground cardamom.

In a shallow baking dish, mix together

olive oil, honey, the ground spices, and some crushed rock sugar.

Place chicken in dish, cover, and marinate for 2-3 hours or overnight.

To make salad: Cut tomatoes, papaya, and kiwi into ¼-inch dice. Add scallions,

138

olive oil, and lemon juice. Season with salt and pepper to taste.

To make hominy cakes: Mix flour, grits, and salt together. In a separate bowl, mix together eggs, milk, water, butter, and oil. Combine wet and dry mixtures. Let sit for 15 minutes.

In a large sauté pan, heat 1 tablespoon oil over medium heat. Add ⅓ cup batter. Cook cake until golden brown, about 1 minute. Flip cake, and continue cooking for one more minute. Continue making cakes until the batter is used up.

To prepare chicken: Preheat oven to 450° F. With a saw, cut sugar cane into 6 pencil-thin "spits." Season chickens with salt and pepper. Wrap each chicken half around a spit, using toothpicks if needed. Place chickens in baking pan and cook for 15 minutes, or until juices run clear when pierced with a fork.

To assemble: On 6 individual plates, first place a hominy cake, then the fruit salad, a piece of chicken, and top with baby greens.

$\mathcal{M}$atzoh Brei with Wild Mushrooms

Serves 6

Matzoh brei is a traditional Passover dish with many variations.
∞

1	cup (2 sticks) plus 2 tablespoons sweet butter	9	large eggs
3	large Spanish onions peeled and minced	¾	cup milk
½	cup vegetable oil	9	sheets plain, unsalted matzoh
6	cups sliced mushrooms (wild or domestic)	6	cups warm water
		⅜	cup chopped parsley
			Salt & freshly ground black pepper

In a large sauté pan, melt 1½ sticks butter over medium heat. Add onions and cook slowly until caramelized, about 30 minutes. Remove from pan and set aside.

In the same pan, heat vegetable oil. Add mushrooms and sauté. Season with salt and pepper to taste. Remove from pan and set aside.

Beat eggs and milk together. Season with salt and pepper. Soak matzoh briefly in water, about 30 seconds, then crumble matzoh into egg mixture.

In the sauté pan, heat the remaining 6 tablespoons butter over medium-high heat. Add matzoh, mushrooms, and onions and stir until slightly crispy. Season with salt and pepper to taste. Stir in chopped parsley. Serve hot.

$\mathcal{S}$hortcake with Warm Berry Compote & Strawberry Ice Cream

Serves 6

Fresh berries bursting with flavor, combined with heavenly biscuits and ice cream—to me, this shortcake's the best.
∞

SHORTCAKE

3¼	cups all-purpose flour
¼	cup cornmeal
2	tablespoons baking powder
½	teaspoon salt
4	tablespoons sugar
½	cup (1 stick) cold butter
2	cups heavy cream, plus extra for tops
	Confectioners' sugar for dusting

COMPOTE

¼	cup water
½	cup sugar
1	tablespoon fresh lemon juice
3	cups mixed berries (strawberries, blueberries, blackberries, etc.)
3	tablespoons sweet butter
1	tablespoon grated lemon zest
1	cup heavy cream
1	pint strawberry ice cream

To make shortcake: In a large bowl, mix dry ingredients together. Cut in butter, until mixture is the texture of coarse cornmeal. Slowly pour in cream and mix lightly. Chill for 30 minutes.

Preheat oven to 325° F. On a floured work surface, roll dough to a 1-inch thickness. Cut into 3-inch circles with a biscuit cutter. Place on parchment-lined cookie sheets. Brush tops of biscuit with cream. Bake for 20 minutes, or until golden. When biscuits are cool, split them horizontally.

To make compote: In a large saucepan, bring water and sugar to a boil over high heat. Reduce heat to low. Add lemon juice and berries and heat for a few minutes until just warmed through. Remove from heat. Gently stir in butter and lemon zest.

To serve: Heat shortcakes until warm and toasty. Spoon warm fruit onto 6 dessert plates. Place bottom half of

shortcake on top of fruit. Top with ice cream, then whipped cream. Cover with shortcake top. Dust with sugar and serve immediately.

Mary Sue Milliken &

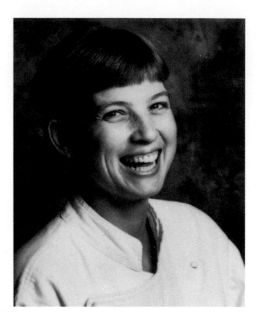

T HEY HAVE BEEN PARTNERS in the kitchen for fifteen years—a remarkable phenomenon in the competitive kitchens of today's top restaurants. Mary Sue Milliken and Susan Feniger, co-owners and chefs at Border Grill in Santa Monica, California, are two of the bright lights of the new California cuisine. Their careers have been entwined from the beginning. In fact, both of these native midwesterners got their start making doughnuts during their high school years.

After finishing cooking school in 1977, Milliken set her sights on working at Le Perroquet, what she considered to be the best restaurant in Chicago at the time. She landed an interview with owner Jovan Treboyevic, who told her, "It would create havoc to have a pretty young thing like you in my kitchen." Milliken launched a vigorous campaign for the job, writing him every other day and calling once a week. After six weeks he broke down and hired her—she was the first woman chef at the restaurant. Milliken says, "I remember him being pleased that I was so gung-ho. My hair was short, I had steel-toed shoes, and I never asked for help. I was a completely autonomous overachiever." Milliken was forever inspired by the innovative food—using American and seasonal ingredients in light and imaginative ways—coming out of Le Perroquet in the late '70s. She credits Treboyevic as her mentor and guide throughout her career.

Two months after Milliken began her job at Le Perroquet, another woman was begging Treboyevic for a job. He told Milliken, "You worked out so well I'm going to try another girl." The other girl was Susan Feniger, who came to Le Perroquet by way of Toledo, Ohio, and the Culinary Institute of America. When the chef at Le Perroquet went on vacation, the two women were left to run the kitchen for three weeks. They were young and nervous but handled it all superbly. For both it was an empowering experience, but after a year together they each moved on to other pursuits.

In 1980 came another serendipitous meeting for these two who were clearly destined to make beautiful food together. Milliken was leaving for France to continue her culinary education when she learned that Feniger, too, was planning to spend a year abroad. They landed in Paris within a day of each other. Before leaving France they spent a month together—prowling the markets, cooking together, and, over a bottle of wine or two, talking about opening a restaurant, Feniger recalls. Even though they were virtually penniless, they would dream about what they would call their restaurant and what would be on the menu.

After Paris, Milliken returned to Chicago and Feniger headed to Los Angeles.

Greek Revival

Grilled Mussels
with
Sumac Mayonnaise

———

Baked Feta
on Herb Salad

———

Fillets of Snapper
Wrapped in
Grape Leaves

———

Roasted Eggplant &
Mashed Potatoes

———

Blanched Escarole

———

Lemon-Peppermint
Ice Cream

———

Honey-Soaked Cookies

———

Hot Mint Tea

SAUVIGNON BLANC
Kenwood
or
Morgan

Susan Feniger

Feniger was cooking for a little café and urged Milliken to come for a visit. Milliken arrived to find a tiny 10 x 10-foot kitchen with two hot plates and no oven. She was determined not to like California, and certainly didn't want to live there, but when the café's special one night was "calf's tongue with lobster sauce and pears" she realized, "They'll do and eat anything out here. It was so wild I couldn't believe it." Thoughts of the fabulous possibilities for food sealed her fate, and in 1981 Milliken moved to California to work with Feniger at City Cafe.

They characterize their cooking as "rustic, hearty cuisine with strong bold flavors." Both have always been drawn to peasant-style food, and in their first months cooking together this interest took the form of country French cuisine. They started out making their own pastries, then gradually replaced items that were coming from other suppliers with their own versions of pâtés, pickles, and smoked meats. Their food evolved as their horizons broadened. Feniger's travels to India brought vegetable fritters, curries, raitas, and chutneys to the menu. Milliken's trips to Thailand added new Asian influences. Although they like to soak up the ideas of other cultures, they don't like to mix them up, Milliken says. For instance she wouldn't use lemongrass in any recipe other than in a Thai dish.

All of this interesting and eclectic food drew praise from customers and media alike. Julia Child came to visit—and hit her head on the hood in the tiny kitchen. They opened City Restaurant and converted the café into the original Border Grill. Since

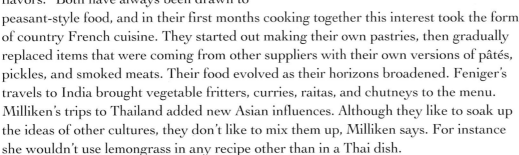

1990, Milliken and Feniger have been working their magic with Latin food, drawing on dishes with origins in Mexico, Guatemala, and Brazil.

In talking with Susan Feniger and Mary Sue Milliken, the satisfaction and enjoyment they derive from working with each other and making great food together is palpable. "We truly collaborate on most everything. It wouldn't have worked for either of us *not* to have shared the spotlight," Feniger says.

A trip to Greece served as inspiration for this marvelous Mediterranean menu. From the spicy and smoky mussels to the zesty lemon-peppermint ice cream, the perfect pairings of ingredients and flavors are just what you would expect from this real-life dynamic duo.

Grilled Mussels with Sumac Mayonnaise

Serves 6

These delicately smoky mussels are a great beginning for any meal from the grill. Although it was hard to convince us that grilling was a worthy technique for mussels, we've found that even if a few drops of juice are lost, the flavor is divine. If you're not using the grill, these can be made in a red-hot sauté pan with great results too. Grilled wedges of country bread make a nice accompaniment.

∾

MAYONNAISE

- 1 egg yolk
- 1 tablespoon champagne vinegar
- Juice of ½ lemon
- 1 teaspoon salt
- ½ teaspoon freshly ground black pepper
- 3-4 shots hot pepper sauce
- 1-2 cloves garlic, minced
- 1 tablespoon ground sumac (or zest of 1 lemon and 2 teaspoons paprika)
- 1 cup olive oil

MUSSELS

- ¼ cup olive oil
- 1 teaspoon salt
- ½ teaspoon freshly ground black pepper
- 4-6 cloves garlic, minced
- Juice of 2 lemons
- 1 bunch fresh thyme leaves, roughly chopped
- 2 pounds small black mussels, debearded, scrubbed and patted dry

To make mayonnaise: In a small bowl, whisk together egg yolk, vinegar, lemon juice, salt, pepper, hot sauce, garlic, and sumac. Whisking constantly, add olive oil in a steady stream until an emulsion forms. Set aside.

To grill mussels: Prepare a grill. In a large bowl, mix olive oil, salt, pepper, garlic, lemon juice, and thyme. Add mussels and toss to coat well. Place mussels on a very hot grill, leaving any excess marinade in the bowl. Cover mussels with a large pot lid and cook just until the mussels open. Discard any mussels that do not open. Return the mussels to the bowl and toss with the remaining marinade.

To serve: Place mussels with their juice in flat soup plates. Put the reserved sumac mayonnaise in a squirt bottle or use a fork to drizzle thin stripes over the open mussels.

144

Baked Feta on Herb Salad

Serves 6

1½ teaspoons salt
1   teaspoon freshly ground black pepper
½   cup plus 2 tablespoons fruity olive oil
¼   cup red wine vinegar
1   cup Italian parsley leaves
1   cup sweet basil leaves
½   cup fresh mint leaves
2   cups watercress, washed
2   cups mizuna, washed
2   cups lamb's lettuce, washed
    Chives, chervil, and tarragon to taste
1   green bell pepper, roasted, peeled, and seeded
1   yellow bell pepper, roasted, peeled, and seeded
1   red bell pepper, roasted, peeled, and seeded
1   bunch fresh oregano leaves, washed and roughly chopped
12 ounces feta cheese, drained

Preheat broiler or grill.

In a small bowl, whisk together 1 teaspoon of the salt, ½ teaspoon of the pepper, ½ cup of the olive oil, and vinegar. Set aside.

In a large bowl toss together parsley, basil, mint, watercress, mizuna, lamb's lettuce, chives, chervil, and tarragon. Set aside.

Cut roasted peppers into 2-inch julienne strips and place in a medium-sized bowl with oregano, the remaining ½ teaspoon of the salt, ½ teaspoon of the pepper, and 2 tablespoons of the olive oil.

Divide feta into 6 equal slices about ½-inch thick. Place them each on a square of aluminum foil. If using a broiler, place ⅙ of the pepper mixture under each piece of cheese. If using a grill, place the peppers on top. Then wrap the cheese and peppers in the foil, sealing it tightly. Place the six foil packets under the broiler or on the grill for 4-6 minutes or until cheese is hot and melted but not liquefied.

Meanwhile, lightly toss the reserved greens with the dressing and divide the salad evenly among 6 plates.

When cheese is roasted, open the foil packets and place the grilled peppers and feta on the center of each salad so that the peppers are on top of the cheese. Serve immediately.

A salad is only as good as your mix of greens and herbs. We like to add as many different kinds as possible for an elegant and intriguing result. Don't hesitate to create your own favorite combination; you should have 8-9 cups total greens and herbs.

Fillets of Snapper Wrapped in Grape Leaves

Serves 6

4	cups yogurt
8	pickling cucumbers
⅓	cup sun-dried tomatoes
8	cloves garlic, minced
1½	teaspoons salt, plus more for snapper

½	teaspoon freshly ground black pepper, plus more for snapper
2½	pounds skinless, boneless, snapper fillets
1	small jar grape leaves in brine Olive oil for brushing Kalamata olives

Drain yogurt in cheesecloth for 2-4 hours to yield 2 cups.

Peel and grate cucumbers; sprinkle with salt. Place in a colander to drain for 1-2 hours.

Reconstitute tomatoes in 1 cup of boiling water until just softened, 10-12 minutes. Drain and chop roughly. Mix tomatoes, the drained yogurt, the reserved cucumbers, garlic, salt, and pepper. Reserve in the refrigerator until ready to serve.

Preheat broiler or grill to medium-high.

Season snapper evenly with salt and pepper. Brush lightly with olive oil.

Rinse grape leaves thoroughly under running water, then pat dry. Spread 2-3 leaves in overlapping fashion on a work surface. Place a seasoned fillet in the center and wrap the grape leaves around it, entirely enclosing the fish. Set aside. Continue with the other fillets until all the fish have been wrapped.

Grill or broil the wrapped fillets 2-4 minutes per side, or until barely cooked through.

Place a dollop of yogurt sauce on each of 6 plates. Place a wrapped fillet on top of the sauce. Garnish with olives.

Roasted Eggplant & Mashed Potatoes

Serves 6

2 medium eggplants
2 pounds baking potatoes (about 6 medium), peeled and quartered
1 tablespoon salt, plus more to taste
½ cup olive oil
1 cup sour cream
    Freshly ground black pepper

Preheat grill or broiler.

Roast eggplant over a grill or under a broiler for about ½ hour, until well blackened all over and soft throughout. Cool on a plate, saving the juices. When cool enough to handle, remove stem and skin and roughly chop eggplant pulp.

In a large saucepan, cover potatoes with water. Add salt. Bring to a boil. Reduce heat to low; simmer, uncovered, until potatoes are soft, 20-30 minutes.

Drain. While potatoes are still warm, mash with a potato masher or food mill. Keep warm.

In a medium-sized skillet, heat olive oil over low heat. Add the reserved eggplant, cover, and keep warm until ready to use.

In a small skillet, heat sour cream. Fold sour cream and eggplant into the reserved potatoes. Mix well. Season with salt and freshly ground black pepper to taste. Serve immediately.

This zingy version of mashed potatoes is the perfect accompaniment to any Mediterranean meal.

Blanched Escarole

Serves 6

2 heads escarole, washed, cored, leaves separated
½ cup extra virgin olive oil
    Juice of 2 limes
1 teaspoon salt
½ teaspoon freshly ground black pepper

Bring a large pot of salted water to a boil. Add escarole leaves. Cook 2-3 minutes. Drain well, squeezing out excess water.

In a large bowl, whisk together olive oil, lime juice, salt and pepper. Add hot escarole. Toss gently and serve immediately.

This underused green prepared in this fashion is typical of a dish we ate on one inspirational trip to Greece. Any greens will work well. The key to the success of this dish is in cooking the greens quickly in plenty of boiling water to remove any bitterness.

Lemon-Peppermint Ice Cream

Serves 6

7 lemons, scrubbed with warm water	2 cups half-and-half
9 egg yolks	1½ cups cream
1 cup sugar	2 teaspoons pure vanilla extract
2 bunches fresh peppermint leaves	

We have been making this lemon ice cream for over a decade but only recently discovered that fresh mint steeped in the cream makes it even more delicious. If you have an herb garden, you've experienced mint's abundance. Both this ice cream and the hot mint tea are great ways to use it up.

Remove zest from lemons, being careful not to get any of the white pith. Set zest aside. Juice enough lemons (probably 4) to make 1 cup lemon juice. Set juice aside.

In a large bowl, vigorously whisk yolks, lemon zest, and sugar until lemon-colored. Meanwhile, in a medium-sized saucepan bring peppermint, half-and-half, and cream to a full rolling boil. Immediately whisk into the yolk mixture. Strain and add vanilla and lemon juice. Let cool.

Process according to the ice cream maker's manufacturer's instructions. Freeze until set, 2-4 hours.

To serve, scoop into chilled ice cream dishes, and pass the honey cookies (recipe opposite).

Honey-Soaked Cookies

Makes 4 dozen cookies

1½ cups corn oil
1   cup (2 sticks) unsalted butter, softened
2¾ cups sugar
    Juice and zest of ½ orange
2   teaspoons baking powder

1   teaspoon baking soda
4   cups all-purpose flour, plus more to make a medium dough
1   cup honey
1½ cups water
¾   cup chopped walnuts

Preheat the oven to 325° F. Lightly grease a baking sheet.

In a large mixing bowl, beat oil and butter until creamy. Add ¾ cup of the sugar and continue beating until thoroughly combined. Stir in orange juice and zest, mixing well.

In a small bowl, combine baking powder, baking soda, and 1 cup of the flour.

Add the flour mixture to the oil mixture. Then add the remaining 3 cups of the flour, a little at a time, thoroughly mixing after each addition, until a medium dough is formed. Dough should hold its shape without spreading.

Shape by teaspoonsful into ovals about 2 inches long and place on the prepared baking sheet. Bake 15-20 minutes, until cookies are firm and only very lightly browned. Cool on wire racks.

To make syrup: Meanwhile, in a small saucepan, boil the remaining 2 cups of the sugar, honey, and water for 2-3 minutes. Reduce heat. While the syrup is gently simmering, dip the cooled cookies in the hot syrup for a moment or two, making sure all sides are covered. Remove cookies with slotted spoon. Sprinkle immediately with walnuts.

Dry on rack. Place in paper cups to serve.

These cookies are incredibly addictive. I fell in love with them when I was just a tot helping my Aunt Georgia make traditional Greek holiday treats. They're the perfect accompaniment for the tart, refreshing Lemon-Peppermint Ice Cream.

Hot Mint Tea

Serves 8

2   bunches fresh mint leaves
    Lemon wedges

Honey to taste

Wash mint leaves and place in a large teapot.

Bring 8 cups freshly drawn cold water to a full rolling boil. Pour over the mint.

Close teapot and steep 4-6 minutes.

Serve immediately with lemon wedges and honey.

Odessa Piper

I WAS FORTUNATE TO GROW UP in a family where many activities centered around food. My dad would take me hunting for wild mushrooms, or the whole family would go to Maine and pick wild blueberries that would be used throughout the year in pancakes and muffins. I think it's important to get children involved in gardening and actually raising and procuring food themselves."

It seems that this early foraging for food made quite an impression on Odessa Piper. For most of her life she has been an advocate of sustainable agriculture, and for the last twenty years she has been interpreting the heartland's finest regional ingredients into exquisite seasonal menus at L'Etoile, her Madison, Wisconsin, restaurant.

In the late '60s Piper joined a commune that was dedicated to sustainable farming—eating only what was raised on the farm. She says this experience was instrumental in developing her credo of cooking from available seasonal ingredients, even in the winter months.

When she moved to Madison in 1971, Piper became totally enthralled with the diversity and quality of the food in the region. She was living on a farm that was the primary supplier for a restaurant that was going to serve only organic food—a new concept at the time. She eventually landed her first restaurant job there. Several years later, when the opportunity arose to buy a restaurant, she started L'Etoile.

Piper has developed strong ties to local farmers and can be found every Saturday filling her wagon at the Madison Farmer's Market. "I take an inordinate amount of time by most restaurant standards in procuring ingredients." And it shows, in the pride and reverence she takes in devising the perfect recipe to make each ingredient shine. Every season presents new opportunities—in the spring, baked morels are filled with pheasant pâté, and the first strawberries from Harmony Valley Farm are served with pralines and cream. In the summer, fresh goat cheese is baked in a squash blossom, and brambleberry crêpes are filled with wild blackberry ice cream. The autumn harvest brings Moonglow pears to be poached in wine, or cider syrup for special sauces. Come winter, 50 percent of the menu is dedicated to ingredients that have been preserved. "It's important to show we don't have to roll over and play dead when winter comes," Piper says. Cherries, blueberries, and cranberries will be dried and used in the winter for a savory fruit strudel served with venison. She will seek out colorful winter-keeping vegetables, like the beauty heart radish, that can make any dish festive.

This winter menu reflects the Midwestern bounty that is so magical for Odessa Piper.

Seared Ahi Tuna with Pumpkin Seed Oil, Pumpkin Seeds & Sprouts

Serves 6

12 ounces sushi grade tuna
2 tablespoons olive oil plus oil for serving
6 tablespoons roasted, salted, shelled pumpkin or sunflower seeds, pulverized

6 tablespoons pumpkin seed oil
1 tablespoon white balsamic or other high quality white wine vinegar
1½ cups sunflower sprouts
3 tablespoons shelled pumpkin seeds (pepitas)

Brush tuna with 1 tablespoon of the olive oil and season with salt and pepper. In a cast iron skillet, grill or sear tuna for a few seconds on both sides to make a thin crust. Brush the tuna again with olive oil and press both sides of the tuna into pulverized pumpkin seeds. Wrap tightly in plastic film, weight to press the seeds into the crust, and refrigerate.

To assemble: Chill 6 large plates. Zigzag a drizzle of olive oil over each plate, then overlap with the pumpkin oil to create a wavy abstract on the plate. Dot plate with drops of vinegar (about ⅓ teaspoon each). Cut thin slices (¼ inch-⅛ inch) off the chilled tuna. Place some sprouts off center of each plate and fan the tuna

slices around it. Sprinkle with kosher salt and scatter more seeds over plate.

On a wine-buying trip to Austria, I found a cold-pressed Styrian pumpkin seed oil. Its flavor alone would be cause enough to lug it home, but its emerald green color captivated me. Cold-pressed pumpkin seed oil is available in specialty stores. I add crispy seeds and succulent sprouts to enhance the oil's octaves.

I make this entrée around the winter holidays, when venison is plentiful and inspiration can be found in the root cellar. A local farm grows a winter-keeping radish for us called beauty heart. It has a deep scarlet center and green exterior.

$\mathcal{V}$enison Tenderloin with Horseradish Compound Butter & Seared Winter Greens

Serves 6

COMPOUND BUTTER

- 1 small beauty heart (or other) radish
- ½ cup (1 stick) unsalted butter, softened
- 1 tablespoon minced shallots
- 1 tablespoon chopped parsley
- 2 tablespoons coarsely grated fresh horseradish root
- ¼ teaspoon salt plus 2 pinches
- ¼ teaspoon freshly ground black pepper
- 1 tablespoon lemon juice

VENISON & SAUCE

- 2-3 venison tenderloins
    Olive oil for searing
- 3 tablespoons butter
- ¾ cup minced onions
- ½ cup plus 1 tablespoon Worcestershire sauce
- 3 cups beef or venison demi-glace
    Salt & freshly ground black pepper

GREENS

- 1½ tablespoons oil
- 1 medium onion, minced
- 4½ cups red Swiss chard
- 4½ cups kale
- 4½ cups spinach

roll out to a log 2 inches in diameter. Chill for at least 3 hours. Just prior to serving slice compound butter into ¼-inch thick rounds, peel off paper and soften to room temperature.

To prepare venison: Preheat oven to 400° F. Trim, salt, and pepper venisons. (Sizes will vary but you can usually expect to get 2-4 portions per tenderloin.) In a very hot sauté pan with a little oil, sear tenderloins to keep meat from sticking. Finish tenderloins in oven for about 5-7 minutes until medium rare. Let meat rest for 2 minutes before slicing.

While tenderloins are finishing, add 3 tablespoons butter and onions to the pan and reduce flame to sweat the onions. Add Worcestershire and demi-glace, reduce slightly until flavors combine. Add salt and pepper to taste.

To make compound butter: Cut radish into matchsticks. In a small saucepan over high heat, poach briefly, chill, pat dry, and dice. Place all ingredients except radish in a mixing bowl and combine thoroughly. Add radish to mixture. Mound onto a piece of wax paper and

To make greens: In a large skillet, heat oil and sauté the onions. Increase heat, toss in greens, and, using tongs, turn to coat with oil and slightly wilt. Season with salt and pepper.

To serve: Tightly mound and center greens and mashed potatoes (page 154) on warmed plates. Slice venison thinly and fan out. Save juices and spoon over venison. Place slices of compound butter to melt over the sliced venison. Spoon sauce at base of venison and serve.

L'Etoile's Wild Rice & Shiitake Mushroom Soup

Serves 6-8

1 cup uncooked wild rice	1 onion
4 cups water	4 cloves garlic, cut in quarters
¼ teaspoon salt	Handful of parsley stems
	4 sprigs fresh thyme
VEGETABLE STOCK	2 crushed bay leaves
2 carrots	2 cups shiitake mushroom stems
2 turnips	2 tablespoons white beans
2 burdock roots	2 cups dry white wine
1 celery root	6 cracked peppercorns
2 leeks (green part)	3-4 cups thinly sliced shiitake
1 fennel bulb's top stem and weed	mushroom caps

In a saucepan, bring rice, water, and salt to a boil. Stir, reduce heat to a simmer, cover and cook for 40-45 minutes just until rice kernels puff open. Do not overcook. Drain off the excess liquid to use in the vegetable stock.

Slice first twelve stock ingredients into roughly inch-long pieces. Place in a stockpot, add the broth drained from the wild rice, white beans and 6 cups of water, or enough to just cover the vegetables. Bring to a boil, cover, reduce heat to low and simmer for 40 minutes. Add wine and peppercorns. Cook for 15 minutes more.

Strain through medium mesh strainer, pushing the softened vegetables through with the back of the ladle to slightly thicken the broth.

Cool and season with salt to taste.

To serve: Heat a thin layer of oil in a large sauté pan over high heat. Cook mushroom slices in a single layer just until the edges turn golden and crispy. Return the sautéed mushrooms to a large saucepan and add 1 cup of broth and ⅓ cup of wild rice for each portion you are planning to serve. Bring to a boil and simmer for a full minute. Distribute broth, rice and mushrooms evenly into warmed bowls.

Some enterprising farmers in the Midwest are growing shiitakes year-round so we have a steady winter supply of the mushrooms, root vegetables, and wild rice that this soup calls for. The delicate broth highlights the meaty flavor of the shiitakes. This soup also works well with a mushroom or chicken stock.

☙

Peppercorn-Sour Cream Mashed Potatoes

Serves 6

6 potatoes
½ cup sour cream
½ cup melted butter

2 teaspoons fresh cracked black peppercorns

Boil potatoes in salted water until tender. Drain, let cool slightly and peel. Add sour cream, butter, and pepper. Mash but do not overmix. Adjust flavor with salt, if needed.

Persimmon Pastry Purse
Filled with Hickory Nut Penuche

Serves 6

1 cup hickory nuts (or pecans)
14 tablespoons unsalted butter
1 cup light brown sugar
¼ cup milk
   Pinch of salt
1 cup confectioners' sugar

1 tablespoon sugar
6 sheets phyllo dough
   (12 x 17-inch size)
3 ripe Fuyu persimmons
2-4 tablespoons milk

Preheat oven to 300° F.

In a pie plate, toss nuts in ½ teaspoon vegetable oil and 3 pinches of salt. Lightly toast nuts for 10 minutes.

In a small saucepan bring 8 table-spoons butter, brown sugar, ¼ cup milk, and salt to a boil. Reduce heat to medium and continue to boil, stirring constantly for 1 minute. Remove from heat.

Add confectioners' sugar to mixture, stir until blended, then add ¾ cup of the hickory nuts. This mixture handles best when still warm. If it stiffens up, reheat with 1-2 teaspoons milk until malleable.

Pulverize the remaining ¼ cup of the hickory nuts with 1 tablespoon sugar.

In a small saucepan melt remaining 6 tablespoons of butter.

To assemble: Preheat oven to 350° F. Keep phyllo covered with plastic wrap so it won't turn brittle.

Place one phyllo sheet on a clean, dry work surface. Brush a light layer of butter over the entire surface, starting first with the edges. Place a second sheet on top of the first. Repeat brushing with butter and sprinkle a bit of the pulverized hickory nut mixture over the sheet. Place a third sheet down and repeat the butter and nuts procedure. Cut the buttered stack with scissors or pizza cutter into

154

6 even squares by making a grid of one cut along the length and three cuts along the width. Then place one square on top of another, offsetting its corner so that the stack has 8 points. Repeat with other squares to make three stacks. Place half a persimmon in the center of each stack. Place a heaping tablespoon of the hickory nut penuche in the center of each persimmon. Gather up the edges of the phyllo square to close around the filled persimmon like a purse and spread the edges out for a jaunty effect. Brush the outside of the purse completely with melted butter. Repeat procedure to make the other three purses.

Transfer purses to a cookie sheet. Refrigerate for 15 minutes to set the phyllo into its purse shape. Then bake for 15-20 minutes or until golden all over. Remelt the remaining penuche with 2-4 tablespoons milk until it is spreadable. Dust the purse with confectioners' sugar and serve warm with crème anglaise feathered with the remaining penuche.

Crème Anglaise

2 cups heavy cream
⅓ cup sugar
½ vanilla bean split lengthwise
5 medium egg yolks, lightly whisked

In a heavy-bottomed saucepan, combine cream, sugar, and vanilla bean. Bring to a simmer while stirring to dissolve sugar and soften vanilla bean. Scrape vanilla seeds into the cream.

Bring the cream to a full boil, remove from heat. Whisk some of the hot cream into the egg yolks, then immediately turn the tempered yolks back into the cream and stir constantly with a rubber spatula, letting the heat of the pan finish the thickening. When thick (about 15-30 seconds) immediately pour the anglaise through a fine sieve, cover surface with a piece of plastic wrap, and chill.

The way we make this sauce might give some people pause, but I find it more trustworthy than heating the eggs and cream gradually. Our method requires a heavy-gauge pot to retain heat, which sets up the custard in less than a minute.

Elka Gilmore

MY MOTHER WAS A BAD COOK, so we went out to eat a lot. She wasn't a meat-loaf-with-ketchup kind of cook, but she would try to make things like octopus in spaghetti sauce—often with disastrous results." These frequent trips to restaurants shaped Elka Gilmore's impressions of dining, and early on she decided to pursue the culinary arts. Growing up in Texas, Gilmore worked as a dishwasher at age eleven, and later as a cook and baker. Gilmore says everything about the restaurant environment was intoxicating to her.

"I never did go to culinary school, but I feel like I'm still in the process of one long apprenticeship twenty-three years later." Her first real job as a chef was at Odessa Piper's restaurant in Madison, Wisconsin— Gilmore was only sixteen. She later became recognized as one of the top chefs in in California, working both in Los Angeles and San Francisco, most recently at the notable Liberté and at Elka's.

In 1995 Gilmore moved to New York to become executive chef at Kokachin, the cutting-edge Asian seafood restaurant in the Omni Berkshire Place Hotel. She considers the sixty chefs who work for her to be among her mentors. "I've always gotten a lot of energy out of the people I've worked with, either as peers or subordinates. Each one of my chefs is a mentor to me in the sense that I grow every day from being able to work with them and observe their style."

In talking about her cooking, Gilmore says the raw product is of primary importance to her—well over 50 percent of her total energy goes into sourcing. "My

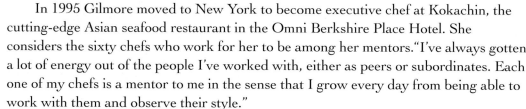

cooking has to be very flexible because when you only accept the very best, it means that you often end up rejecting quite a bit in the course of a day. So if you were planning on a mango sauce, you'd better be prepared to move to passion fruit." She says she tries to cook in a way that's reverent to the pristine quality of the ingredients.

Although some of her dishes may seem exotic, Gilmore says, "I tend to use simple elements combined in ways that complement each other. I'll use traditional flavor combinations but in unusual presentations, or with products you wouldn't think of."

Gilmore's elegant menu may require a trip to the Asian market for items like wasabi, ginger oil, shiso leaves, mirin, and nori, but the very special dishes that result will be well worth it.

156

Ahi Tuna Tartare on Nori Rounds

Serves 4

NORI ROUNDS

1 cup sushi rice, cooked and sprinkled with rice wine vinegar

2 sheets nori

1 teaspoon wasabi (Japanese horseradish)

TUNA

½ pound (#1 quality) sashimi Ahi tuna, cut into ¼-inch pieces

2 tablespoons peeled, seeded, finely chopped cucumbers

2 tablespoons finely chopped scallions

1 teaspoon grated fresh ginger

1 teaspoon mirin (Japanese cooking wine)

Dash sesame oil

Salt & freshly ground black pepper

Daikon radish sprouts

To make nori rounds: Lightly toast nori sheets over gas flame. Lay one sheet on a bamboo sushi mat and spread evenly with half of the rice, leaving ½-inch on each end. Spread half the wasabi down the center of the rice. Repeat with the other nori roll. Roll into 1-inch diameter rolls, cut into 24 half-inch rounds.

To prepare tuna: In a large bowl, mix together tuna, cucumbers, scallions, ginger, mirin, sesame oil, and salt and pepper to taste. Mound on top of the nori rounds. Garnish with radish sprouts and serve immediately.

Elegant as an appetizer or at a party. It's important that you use the finest quality tuna as it is essentially eaten raw. Nori are the thin sheets of dried seaweed that are used to wrap sushi. You may also serve the tuna on cucumber slices or even potato chips.

157

Lobster with Coconut Peas

Serves 4

4   1-½ pound lobsters, blanched and
    shelled
2   tablespoons unsalted butter
1   tablespoon chopped shallots
1   cup unsweetened coconut milk
1   cup sautéed morel mushrooms
1   tablespoon ginger juice
3   cups shelled peas (3-4 pounds
    unshelled)

   Seven-pepper spice, to taste
2   tablespoons chopped fresh basil
2   tablespoons chopped fresh mint
2   tablespoons chopped scallions
   Juice of one lime
¼   teaspoon salt
2   tablespoons pea shoots

Preheat oven to 450° F.

Place lobster in a shallow pan, season with salt and pepper, and roast for 3-5 minutes. Set aside.

In a large skillet, melt butter over medium heat. Add shallots and sauté until tender. Add coconut milk, morels, ginger juice, and seven-pepper spice and reduce slightly. Add peas, basil, mint, scallions, lime juice, and salt. Cook for about 2 minutes longer until peas are tender. Adjust seasonings.

To serve, place pea mixture on plates and arrange sliced lobster tail and claws in a circular mound on top. Garnish with pea shoots.

Fresh peas, basil, and mint highlight this delicate sauce for the ever-popular lobster. The sauce is also good on salmon or cod. You could vary it further by substituting asparagus for the peas; both celebrate seasonal eating.

Cucumber Salad with Shiso-Marinated Salmon

Serves 4

SALMON

- 1 stalk lemongrass, coarsely chopped
- ½ large piece of fresh ginger, coarsely chopped
- 12 shiso leaves
- Zest of 1 lemon
- 1½ cups sugar
- 1½ cups kosher salt
- 2 pound salmon fillet, deboned
- 1 cup sake

SALAD

- 1 large English cucumber, peeled and thinly sliced
- ½ teaspoon salt
- ¼ cup rice wine vinegar
- 1 teaspoon finely diced shallots
- 1 teaspoon finely diced fresh ginger
- 1 cup ginger oil
- 2 ounces daikon radish sprouts

A versatile dish that works well as a salad. The cucumber salad makes a good garnish for grilled fish, and the salmon may also be used in place of smoked salmon or gravlax in other recipes.

160

To prepare salmon: In a food processor, place lemongrass, ginger, shiso leaves, and lemon zest and process until paste-like, 3-4 minutes.

In a small bowl, mix together sugar and salt.

Place salmon on a work surface, spread sugar-salt mixture over salmon and spread ginger paste on top of sugar-salt mixture. Pour sake over salmon.

Place a cookie-cooling rack on top of a baking sheet pan. Place salmon on top of cooling rack. Cover with another sheet pan and a weight. Let marinate for 2 days in the refrigerator. Remove all the marinade and slice thinly. *(Salmon may be kept covered and refrigerated for up to 5 days.)*

To make salad: In a bowl, marinate cucumbers in salted water for about 30 minutes. In a small bowl, combine rice wine vinegar, shallots, and ginger. Gradually whisk in ginger oil to make a vinaigrette. Dress cucumbers with vinaigrette and place them on a plate in a pattern. Arrange thinly sliced salmon on top. Garnish with daikon sprouts and add a little more vinaigrette.

Fruit Soup

Serves 8-10

3	quarts water
12	ounces blueberries
3	cups sugar
10	ounces lemongrass

¾	cup plus 2 tablespoons lemon juice
1	cinnamon stick
1	teaspoon chopped mint
6	ounces pectin

In a large saucepan, bring all ingredients but pectin to a boil over high heat, then stir in pectin. Shut off flame. Let steep until cool. Strain, then pass through fine strainer 2-3 times. Add berries or other fruit for garnish.

We often serve two small courses of dessert—first a fruit soup, then something chocolate. Leftover soup can be frozen and used at another time.

Donna Katzl

FOR DONNA KATZL, COOKING HAS ALWAYS been therapeutic—literally. In her teens, with her mother very ill, Katzl took on the role of family cook. She found great solace in cooking and preparing elaborate meals. She recalls trekking about the ethnic neighborhoods of Los Angeles with her father in search of the most unusual and the best foods. "He was always ready to experiment. We would come home with fresh fish, unusual sausages, breads, and produce from all over the city. I learned at an early age that if you want the best food, you have to be willing to seek it out."

Katzl studied art and pursued a career in show business. She worked as an extra in movies and television—it's safe to say that she is probably the only chef today who has worked as a dancer in Las Vegas and had a bit part on the television comedy "Mr. Ed."

Later in life, Katzl suffered from panic attacks, but found when she was cooking the problem abated. "So I stayed in the kitchen a lot. . . . My love for cooking and food kept me alive through some dark times."

In the 1960s, Katzl and her husband entertained frequently at extravagant dinner parties. Friends encouraged her to find a professional outlet for her culinary talents, and the Katzls soon found themselves running a catering service, deli, and small café in San Francisco.

In 1977 Katzl took her first cooking class with James Beard, and it gave her just the impetus she needed to refine her skills. In the class she became acquainted with Marion Cunningham, who introduced her to Beard. She attended many more classes and Katzl, Beard, and Cunningham became good friends. "James gave me a lot of new food ideas. He changed my whole perspective," she says. Key among those views: "I knew I would never be happy unless I could serve only the very freshest, highest quality food."

In 1983 she opened the Cafe for All Seasons in San Francisco's West Portal neighborhood. She describes the cuisine there as American bistro fare: "Very simple foods, very fresh foods, simply combined." This midwinter menu showcases that approach. The easy preparation minimizes culinary fanfare and lets the vibrant in-season flavors take center stage: lamb, winter vegetables, rosemary-buttermilk bisuits, and California's tangerines and Meyer lemons.

162

Gorgonzola & Chopped Walnut Toasts with Chives

Serves 4-6

4 ounces softened, crumbled Gorgonzola cheese

2 ounces softened, crumbled Oregon blue cheese

3 ounces ricotta, at room temperature
Salt to taste

⅓ cup finely chopped walnuts

¼ cup, plus 2 tablespoons tiny ring-cut chives

18 slices French baguette
Freshly ground black pepper

In a large mixing bowl, mash the three cheeses. Add salt, mix until smooth. Add walnuts and ¼ cup of the chives. Mix until blended. Refrigerate for at least 2 hours or overnight.

Preheat oven to 250° F. Cut baguette diagonally into 2½-3-inch-thick slices.

Toast in oven 15-20 minutes, until slightly golden and just crisp.

Spread about 2 tablespoons of cheese mixture on each toast. Arrange the toasts on a plate and sprinkle with the remaining 2 tablespoons of the chives and a pinch of coarsely ground pepper.

Three cheeses blend to feature the walnut flavor in this simple appetizer. Perched on a baguette, it's finger food at its best.

Lamb & Vegetable Orzotto

Serves 6

2 tablespoons olive oil
12 ounces lamb steak, coarsely chopped
4 tablespoons unsalted butter
½ cup minced yellow onions
1 tablespoon minced garlic
1 cup white wine
2 cups orzo

6-8 cups hot chicken stock
1 large red bell pepper, roasted, peeled, and finely chopped
⅓ cup chopped parsley
Salt to taste
½ cup grated Asiago cheese

In a medium-sized skillet, heat olive oil. Add lamb, cook till lightly golden. With a slotted spoon, remove lamb and drain.

In a large heavy saucepan, melt 2 tablespoons of the butter over medium-low heat. Add onions and garlic and cook until softened, 2-3 minutes. Add lamb and wine, cook until reduced by half, 3-4 minutes.

Stir in orzo and coat evenly. Add 2 cups of hot chicken stock and cook, stirring until absorbed, 5-6 minutes.

Continue to add as much stock as needed, 1 cup at a time, until orzo is creamy and tender but still firm in center. This process should take 15-18 minutes from the time you first add stock.

Remove from heat and stir in remaining 2 tablespoons of the butter, red pepper, ¼ cup of the parsley, and salt.

Serve individually or on a platter. Sprinkle with grated Asiago cheese and remaining parsley.

Rosemary Buttermilk Biscuits

Makes 16 biscuits

2 cups all-purpose flour
½ teaspoon salt
2 teaspoons baking powder
½ teaspoon baking soda

4 teaspoons ground fresh rosemary
1 tablespoon sugar
½ cup vegetable shortening
⅔ cup buttermilk

Preheat oven to 425° F. Grease two 8-inch cake pans.

In a large mixing bowl, combine flour, salt, baking powder, baking soda, rosemary, and sugar. Mix shortening into the flour mixture until it resembles coarse meal. Add buttermilk all at once and stir just until the dough forms a

ball around a fork. Turn the dough onto a lightly floured board and knead 14 times. Pat until ½-inch thick. Cut into rounds with a 2-inch cookie cutter or glass.

Place biscuits touching each other in the pans and bake for 15-20 minutes. Serve warm with butter.

Butterhead Lettuce Salad
with Roasted Garlic-Honey Dressing

Serves 4-6

This refreshing salad is especially nice in the fall because of the interplay of bacon, spinach, cider, honey, and mustard.

DRESSING
- 1 head garlic
- 7 tablespoons olive oil
- 1 tablespoon Dijonnaise mustard
- 1½ tablespoons Dijon mustard
- 4 tablespoons cider vinegar
- 1 tablespoon honey
- 2 tablespoons water
  Salt to taste

- 1 large butterhead lettuce, washed, dried, and torn
- 3 ounces baby spinach leaves stemmed removed, washed, and dried
- ¼ cup scallions, green part only, thinly sliced
- ⅓ pound thinly cut bacon, fried golden and drained
- ½ cup pine nuts, lightly toasted

Preheat oven to 350° F.

Place entire head of garlic in a small casserole dish. Pour 3 tablespoons olive oil over the garlic and bake for 1 hour.

Let cool completely. In a small bowl, squeeze the garlic out of the skin of each clove and mash.

In a jar, combine the garlic pulp, the remaining 4 tablespoons of olive oil, mustards, vinegar, honey, and water. Mix well. Refrigerate for at least 2 hours to blend flavors.

In a large salad bowl, combine lettuce, spinach, and scallions and refrigerate.

Just before serving, add half of the bacon and pine nuts, and toss with dressing. Serve on individual salad plates and sprinkle each with bacon and pine nuts.

Meyer Lemon-Tangerine Pudding

Serves 6

2 tablespoons unsalted butter, softened
⅞ cup sugar
3 large eggs, separated
1 cup buttermilk

1½ tablespoons all-purpose flour
⅓ cup Meyer lemon juice
Finely grated zest of 1 tangerine
¾ cup whipping cream
1-2 teaspoons sugar

Preheat oven to 350° F.

In a mixing bowl, beat butter until soft. Add sugar, beating until incorporated. Beat in the egg yolks one at a time. Add buttermilk, flour, lemon juice, and tangerine zest. Beat until mixed well, although the mixture may look curdled.

In a small bowl, beat the egg whites at high speed until they form soft peaks. Fold the whites into the batter. Turn into a greased 1½ quart baking dish and set it in a pan of hot water that comes halfway up the sides of the dish.

Bake for 45-50 minutes. Let cool.

In a small chilled bowl, whip cream and sugar together until soft and fluffy.

Serve at room temperature or chilled, topped with a spoonful of softly whipped cream.

A little twist on a classic lemon pudding. The Meyer lemon is native to California. If Meyer lemons are not available, you may substitute regular lemon juice.

Jody Adams

L IKE MOST OF HER CULINARY COMPATRIOTS, Jody Adams has always cooked. Growing up in Providence, Rhode Island, she was heavily influenced by that city's Italian culture, "although I am a WASP through and through," she says. During her teen years her family spent time in Europe, and there Adams was introduced to many new foods and ways of eating. Today her cuisine reflects these early experiences. As one of Boston's top chefs for over a decade, she is known for her ingenuity in giving Italian dishes her own innovative twists—as evidenced in this tantalizing contemporary Italian menu.

During high school Adams worked for Nancy Verde-Barr who then taught cooking classes. It was Verde-Barr, now Julia Child's executive chef, who set Adams on her current course and helped her transform her home-cooking interest into a career by teaching her the fundamentals of French and Italian classic cooking technique.

Adams moved to Boston in the early '80s and landed at job at Seasons Restaurant. It was one of the cutting-edge restaurants in the city, if not the country—Lydia Shire was the chef and Gordon Hamersley was sous-chef. Under the tutelage of these culinary giants, Adams was introduced to restaurant cooking. Although the restaurant emphasized traditional techniques, there were ingredients Adams had never seen before, and she learned about cuisines that were totally new to her. "Fusion cooking" was not yet a buzzword, but essentially that's what Adams was doing. When Hamersley left Seasons to open his first restaurant, Adams went along as sous-chef—she did everything from working on the line to butchering.

Since 1994, Adams has been executive chef at Rialto in Cambridge, where the menu is inspired by the food of France, Italy, and Spain. At this point in her career she feels she has developed an instinct for creating new dishes and menus. "I cook from my heart and from my mouth; I don't cook from my head," she observes. "I cook from tradition, using combinations of ingredients that make sense and go together. It's smart cooking—not gimmicky at all. Anything that's on the plate is there because it's an integral part of what's going to happen when you put the food in your mouth—not because it looks pretty."

Spicy Marinated Salmon with a Parsley & Spinach Salad

Serves 4

2   cloves garlic, thinly sliced
1   serrano pepper, seeded, thinly sliced, and soaked in cold water
3   tablespoons fresh lemon juice
6   tablespoons extra virgin olive oil
    Salt & freshly ground black pepper
1   pound fresh salmon fillet, skinned and boned

¼   cup Italian parsley leaves, washed and dried
1   cup small spinach leaves, washed and trimmed
1   tablespoon toasted pine nuts
1   tablespoon raisins, soaked in water just to cover
1   tablespoon dried cranberries or cherries

This recipe was inspired by a dish of marinated sea bass I had while in Rome several years ago. It's my New England version — salmon from Maine and dried cranberries from Massachusetts.

Bring a small pan of water to boil and season with salt. Add garlic and cook until tender, about 5 minutes. Drain. Drain pepper slices and pat dry. In a small bowl, toss the garlic, peppers, and lemon juice. Whisk in olive oil. Season with salt and pepper to taste.

Slice salmon as thinly as possibly, on the diagonal, as you would smoked salmon. There should be about 16 slices. Set 4 slices in a square on each of 4 serving plates, leaving a space in the middle of the plates. Season the fish with salt and pepper. Drizzle about 1 tablespoon of the vinaigrette over each plate, covering the salmon. Let sit 5 minutes to marinate.

In a medium-sized bowl, toss parsley, spinach, pine nuts, raisins and dried cranberries with the remaining vinaigrette. Divide the salad equally among the four plates, placing it in the center of each square of salmon. Serve immediately.

Pasta Bundles with
Butternut Squash Stuffing & Gorgonzola Sauce

Serves 4 generously

I love these whimsical bundles. They look like wrapped candy or party favors and can be made ahead of time for convenience. Experiment with other stuffings and sauces.

FILLING

- 1 small butternut squash (about 1½ pounds)
  Salt & freshly ground black pepper
- 2 tablespoons unsalted butter
- 2 shallots, minced
- ½ cup grated Asiago or Parmesan cheese
- ¼ cup amaretti crumbs
- 1 teaspoon sage

SAUCE

- 1 cup heavy cream
- ¼ pound Gorgonzola cheese
  Salt & freshly ground black pepper

BUNDLES

- 16 fresh thin pasta sheets, 3 x 4 inches
- 2 tablespoons melted unsalted butter
- 8 fresh sage leaves

To make filling: Preheat oven to 425° F. Split squash in half. Season with salt and pepper to taste. Set, cut side down, on a lightly oiled baking sheet. Roast 30-45 minutes, until tender and golden on the cut side.

Remove and discard the seeds, scoop the squash out of the skin, and mash until smooth. Do not turn off the oven.

Meanwhile, in a large skillet, melt the butter. Add shallots and cook until tender. Add the mashed squash and cook until dry, about 20 minutes. Let cool. Add cheese, amaretti, and sage. Season with salt and pepper to taste.

To make sauce: In a small skillet, heat cream over low heat, until just warmed through but not boiling. Whisk in Gorgonzola. Cook over low heat until the cheese has melted completely, and sauce is thick enough to coat the back of a spoon. If the sauce is too thin, simmer until reduced. Season with salt and pepper to taste and keep warm.

To make bundles: Blanch pasta sheets in 5 quarts of salted boiling water for 60 seconds. Plunge into ice water. Drain. Arrange the sheets on a lightly oiled baking tray. Put a spoonful of the filling in the middle of each sheet. Roll up like a cigar. Twist the ends to look like wrapped candy. Brush with butter.

To serve: Bake the bundles for 6-7 minutes, or until lightly golden. Drizzle with warm Gorgonzola cream and garnish with sage leaves.

Devil-Style Chicken with Ginger
(Poletto alla Diavola)

Serves 4

4   1-pound range chickens, butterflied, with backbone and wing tips removed
2   tablespoons hot red pepper flakes
4   tablespoons chopped fresh ginger
2   tablespoons chopped garlic
    Extra virgin olive oil

2   shallots, thinly sliced
1   cup white wine
2   cups chicken stock
3   tablespoons unsalted butter
½   teaspoon wine vinegar
    Salt & freshly ground black pepper

Rub the birds with oil. Season them with hot red pepper flakes, 3 tablespoons of the ginger, and 1 tablespoon of the garlic. Place the chickens in a large pan, cover tightly, and refrigerate overnight so chicken absorbs seasonings.

Season the chicken with salt. Heat 2 large skillets over medium heat with 2 tablespoons oil in each. Cook the chickens, one at a time, skin-side down, flattened with weights until cooked three quarters of the way through, about 15-20 minutes. Turn the chicken and cook until the skin is crispy and golden brown, about 5-10 minutes more. Transfer the chickens to a platter and keep warm.

In one of the skillets, pour off excess fat, heat 2 tablespoons of the oil with the remaining 1 tablespoon each of the ginger and garlic. Cook until tender. Deglaze the pan with wine and cook until reduced by three quarters. Add stock and cook until reduced by half. Whisk in butter and season with vinegar, and salt and pepper to taste. Pour this sauce over the chicken and serve.

Fricassee of Spaetzle & Swiss Chard

Serves 4

Spaetzle, known as pasta or dumplings, is unbelievably easy to make. Serve it with stews and roasted meats.

SPAETZLE
- ¾ cup unbleached all-purpose flour
- ¼ cup milk
- 1 large egg
- ½ teaspoon salt
- ⅛ teaspoon ground ginger
- ⅛ teaspoon baking powder
- ½ teaspoon chopped chives
- 1 tablespoon vegetable oil

FRICASSEE
- 2 tablespoons unsalted butter
- ⅛ cup thinly sliced white onions
- ½ teaspoon chopped garlic
- 2 cups Swiss chard leaves cut into ¾-inch strips
- 3 tablespoons water
- Salt & freshly ground black pepper
- 1 teaspoon fresh lemon juice
- 2 tablespoons grated Parmesan cheese

To make spaetzle: In a medium-sized bowl, combine flour, milk, egg, salt, ginger, and baking powder. Beat with a mixer until batter is smooth and thick. Fold in the chives.

Meanwhile, bring a large pot of salted water to a boil. With the side of a spatula, push batter through a large-holed colander to form small irregular dumplings in the boiling water. Cook at a rolling boil until dumplings float to the top. Drain, toss with oil, and spread out in a single layer on a baking sheet to cool.

To make fricassee: In a large skillet, heat butter. Add onions and cook until tender, about 3 minutes. Add garlic and cook 2 more minutes. Add Swiss chard and toss well. Add water and cook slowly until tender, 10-15 minutes. Season with salt and pepper to taste. Add the spaetzle and toss until heated through. Toss with lemon juice and Parmesan. Serve immediately.

Roasted Pears
with White Chocolate Zabaione

Serves 4

ZABAIONE

- 4 egg yolks
- ⅓ cup sugar
- ⅓ cup Marsala
- 4 ounces white chocolate, melted and kept warm
- ½ cup heavy cream

PEARS

- 4 Bosc pears, washed, peeled, halved, and cored
- 4 tablespoons melted unsalted butter
- ½ cup sugar
- 2 tablespoons fresh lemon juice
- 2 ounces semisweet chocolate, melted and kept warm

To make zabaione: In a double boiler over low heat, beat yolks, sugar, and Marsala until thick and foamy, about 5 minutes. Remove from heat. Stir in white chocolate and cream. Chill.

To roast pears: Preheat oven to 400° F. Toss pears with butter, sugar, and lemon juice. Arrange cut-side down in a small roasting pan. Roast for 30-35 minutes, or until the pears are tender, caramelized, and golden brown. Keep warm.

Serve chilled zabaione over warm roasted pears. Drizzle with melted semisweet chocolate.

Roasted and grilled fruits are at the base of all my favorite desserts. The cooking brings out and deepens the flavor of the fruits. They can then stand up to a big-flavored sauce like this one with Marsala and white chocolate.

RoxSand Scocos

FIFTEEN YEARS AGO RoxSand Scocos turned in her paintbrush for a wire whisk. The painter and sculptor transferred her skills from the fine arts to the culinary arts, and today she is one of the top proponents of fusion cooking—the blending of techniques and flavors from different cuisines. Her Phoenix restaurant is a haven for adventuresome and appreciative diners.

Scocos was trained in classic French technique at La Varenne School of Cooking in Paris. She moved from her native Michigan to Hawaii in the late '70s, where she opened two restaurants and a catering company on Oahu. There Scocos found a very international community and created a rather global group of her own—about 75 percent of her staff was French, the sous-chef was Moroccan, and her boyfriend was Chinese. Although she was cooking French food, these cross-cultural influences eventually worked their way into her menus.

After seven years in Hawaii, Scocos moved to Arizona where she and her husband opened a small restaurant in Scottsdale. "I wanted to see if my ideas would fly in this marketplace. When we were developing the restaurant words like fusion and cross-cultural cuisine didn't exist. One day I opened a magazine and saw this word fusion and realized there was a name for what I'd been doing all these years!" Scocos is totally committed to what she calls the "culinary collective consciousness." She draws upon a core repertoire from seven cuisines: Asian, French, Italian, Spanish, Moroccan, Native American, and South American. She believes the possible food combinations are endless. The fusion of Hawaiian and Southwestern flavors might take the form of roast pig accompanied by huevos-avocado tostados and conch fritters. A popular Indian/Thai dish at the restaurant is rice tamales with curried lamb and peanut sauce. At a recent dinner featuring native foods, dishes included Anasazi bean and Peruvian potato salad with lavender dressing and ember-roasted buffalo.

In developing new ideas Scocos tries to isolate a flavor or texture or visual concept about the food before she begins cooking. "It's like a floral arrangement—recognizing the balance or lack of balance in what you're doing."

For this intriguing meal, Scocos uses native American juniper berries and gin to marinate delicate rabbit tenderloins, which are served on grilled red pepper polenta and topped by a colorful Middle Eastern salad. The vegetarian main dish features a risotto surrounded by a hearty vegetable soup. And for dessert, a tropical crème brûlée is accompanied by crispy ginger wafers.

$\mathcal{G}$rilled Rabbit Loins with Roasted Red Pepper Polenta & Fattoush Salad

Serves 8

RABBIT

2 cups soybean oil
½ cup fruit vinegar, such as raspberry
½ tablespoon chopped garlic
9 cloves garlic, bruised
4 juniper berries, toasted
½ teaspoon white peppercorns
2 bay leaves
1 ounce gin
8 rabbit tenderloins (2-3 ounces each)

POLENTA

2 tablespoons olive oil
1 onion, finely chopped
2 cloves garlic, minced
Salt & freshly ground black pepper
2 large red bell peppers, roasted, peeled, and chopped
⅓ cup dry white wine
1½ cups coarsely ground cornmeal
1 cup grated Parmesan cheese

SALAD

½-¾ cup cubed polenta (left over from cut rounds)
1 cup fine julienne of romaine lettuce
½ cup finely diced tomatoes
½ cup finely diced cucumber
2 tablespoons finely diced red onion
2 tablespoons finely chopped scallions
2 tablespoons chopped fresh mint
1 tablespoon chopped fresh parsley

VINAIGRETTE

5 tablespoons olive oil
½ tablespoon grated lemon zest
2 tablespoons lemon juice

GARNISH

1 each red, yellow & green bell pepper, finely diced for garnish
1 lemon, peel, removed and cut into thin strips

(continued on next page)

This dish makes a nice first course, or in larger portions a delightful luncheon plate. The delicate flavor of grilled rabbit is a special treat. Fattoush is traditionally a Middle Eastern salad of broken pita bread. Here I have substituted polenta.

To prepare rabbit: In a small saucepan, combine oil, vinegar, chopped garlic, garlic cloves, juniper berries, peppercorns, bay leaves, and gin over low heat. Heat, but do not boil. Allow to cool to room temperature. Place rabbit loins in a nonreactive baking dish and pour marinade over the rabbit. Cover, refrigerate, and marinate for 24 hours.

Prepare a grill. Remove the rabbit from marinade. Grill the meat for about 5 minutes, turning once. Keep warm.

To make polenta: In a large skillet, heat oil over high heat. Add onions and garlic and sauté until translucent. Add salt and pepper to taste. Add red peppers and simmer for 10 minutes. Add wine, simmer until it is cooked off. Set aside.

In a large saucepan over high heat, bring 7 cups salted water to a boil. Add cornmeal in a thin trickle, beating constantly with a whisk. When all the cornmeal has been added, lower the heat to medium, and begin to stir with a wooden spoon. Cook, stirring constantly for 30-40 minutes or until the polenta comes away easily from the sides of the pot. Add the red pepper mixture, stirring well to incorporate. Add Parmesan.

Pour into a sheet pan and cover with plastic wrap, cutting air holes. Refrigerate until completely set up, at least 1 hour.

Cut the polenta into 4-inch rounds. Save scraps for the salad.

Grill the polenta rounds until nicely browned, about 2-3 minutes on each side.

To make vinaigrette: In a small bowl or jar, whisk together the olive oil, lemon zest, and lemon juice.

To make salad: In a large bowl, combine all the salad ingredients and set aside. Just before serving, Lightly toss with vinaigrette.

To assemble: Cut each piece of grilled rabbit on the bias and set each atop a grilled polenta round on a plate. Top with a serving of Fattoush Salad. Garnish by pooling vinaigrette around perimeter of each plate and sprinkling with tricolored bell peppers and julienned zest.

176

Red Wine & Shiitake Risotto with Winter Vegetable Broth

Serves 8

MUSHROOM BROTH

- ¼ cup olive oil
- 4 cloves garlic
- 1 onion, quartered
- 4 cups coarsely chopped mushrooms, including stems
  - Bouquet garni
  - Black peppercorns
  - Pinch kosher salt

VEGETABLE BROTH

- ¼ cup olive oil
  - Salt & freshly ground black pepper

- 1 parsnip, peeled and diced
- 1 small bunch fresh thyme (tied)
- 1 leek (white part only) diced
- 1 cup diced rutabaga or turnip
- 1 cup Brussels sprout leaves
- 1 cup cannellini beans, cooked and drained
- 1 cup peeled, seeded, and diced tomato
- 8 cups mushroom broth
  - Salt & freshly ground black pepper

(continued on next page)

A classic paniscia from Novara, Italy—this recipe merges two dishes—risotto cooked in red wine, and minestrone. In the original dish, the components are mixed together before serving; here they are prepared separately.

ᘒ

(Red Wine & Shiitake Risotto continued)

RISOTTO
- ½ cup olive oil
- 4 cups shiitake mushroom caps, sliced (use stems for broth)
- 2 tablespoons chopped garlic
- 1½ large onions, diced
- ½ cup red wine
- 2 cups Arborio rice
- 6 cups boiling mushroom broth
- 2 cups grated Parmesan cheese, plus more to taste
- ½ cup (1 stick) unsalted butter

  Salt & freshly ground black pepper

  Fresh herb sprigs, such as thyme or rosemary

To make mushroom broth: In a large stockpot, heat olive oil over high heat. Add garlic, onions, and mushrooms and sauté until vegetables are tender. Cover with 15 cups water. Add bouquet garni, peppercorns, and salt. Bring to a boil, Reduce heat and simmer 1-2 hours. Strain.

To make vegetable broth: Meanwhile, in another large stockpot heat olive oil over medium heat. Add parsnips, thyme, leeks, and rutabaga or turnip and sauté until the vegetables are translucent, about 5 minutes. Add Brussels sprouts, beans, and tomatoes and sauté for 1 minute more. Add the 8 cups mushroom broth and simmer while preparing risotto. Season to taste.

To make risotto: In a large pot, heat olive oil over medium heat. Add shiitake caps, garlic, and onions, cover, and steam until translucent, about 1-2 minutes. Remove cover and gently brown vegetables until they turn a rich amber color. Add wine and cook until liquid is reduced by three-quarters. Add rice, increase heat to high, and sauté until rice kernels are glazed. Add 6 cups boiling mushroom broth one ladle at a time, allowing each ladle to cook into rice, stirring continuously. When all the broth has been absorbed and rice is tender, stir in Parmesan and butter. Season with salt and pepper to taste. Risotto will be very creamy.

To serve: Spoon a cup of the risotto into each shallow bowl. Ladle 1 cup of vegetable broth around it. Garnish with fresh herbs and additional Parmesan if desired. Serve piping hot.

Coconut Brûlée with Ginger Wafers

Serves 8

COCONUT BRÛLÉE

1 cup heavy cream
1 cup shredded coconut
1 cup coconut milk
½ cup sugar
10 egg yolks
1 vanilla bean, cut in half lengthwise
1 cup sugar for broiling

GINGER WAFERS

¾ cup sugar
½ cup (1 stick) unsalted butter, softened
4 egg whites
10 tablespoons all-purpose flour
4 teaspoons ground ginger

To make coconut brûlée: In the top of a double boiler, whisk together cream, coconut, coconut milk, sugar, and egg yolks. Scrape the vanilla seeds into mixture and add vanilla bean shell. Place over simmering water, whisking occasionally. When custard is thick enough to heavily coat a spoon, remove from heat and strain. Pour into individual ramekins and chill overnight.

To make wafers: Preheat oven to 325° F.
In a large bowl, beat sugar, butter, and egg whites. Stir in flour and ginger. Let rest at room temperature for 2 hours.
Lightly grease a baking sheet with butter and dust with flour. Drop dough by tablespoonsful onto the pan. Spread with a spatula. Bake for 6-8 minutes, watching closely, until lightly browned.
Let cool on a rack. Once cool, the wafers will become crispy. Store in a cool dry place for no more than 4-6 hours. However, the batter can be made ahead, and refrigerated. Bring to room temperature or spreadable consistency before baking.

To serve: Preheat broiler. Sprinkle 2 tablespoons sugar on each ramekin, broil until sugar has caramelized and is a deep brown. Watch carefully to avoid scorching.
Serve with a stack of wafers.

Here is an elegant twist on the classic crème brûlée found at every restaurant these days.

Garnish with julienned crystallized ginger and/or fresh berries or tropical fruits such as mangoes, bananas, and kiwis.

$\mathcal{L}$indsey Shere

A S THE ELDEST OF FIVE GIRLS, Lindsey Shere always had plenty of opportunity to help out in the kitchen. She remembers baking for the family's Sunday breakfasts when she was nine years old. One year during her teens she did most of the cooking for the family when her mother was ill.

Shere had planned to be a dress designer and was majoring in home economics in junior college. Though she took some food-related courses she decided "when it came to organic chemistry I realized I didn't really want to work that hard at food." She later transferred to U.C. Berkeley where a wonderful French teacher awakened in her an interest in the food and culture of France. This interest would not take a professional turn until Shere's three children were in school.

In the mid-sixties Shere became friends with a neighbor named Alice Waters. When Waters opened Chez Panisse in 1971 she asked Shere to come on board as pastry chef. Shere describes the early, struggling days at the restaurant: "An acquaintance of Alice's wanted her to start a restaurant with him. He said he knew all about the cooking part, and Alice would be hostess. It turned out he didn't know anything about a kitchen, and after three months he left Alice with this very large, ambitious restaurant. It was open from 6 A.M. until midnight and had fifty employees. The restaurant soon went into the hole." And the rest is history.

Shere and her staff of four are responsible for all the sumptuous desserts at Chez Panisse. She finds inspiration in her large collection of cookbooks and magazines. "I start reading and thinking about what has been done before. I find that helps me remember things I've not thought about for a while. There are so many categories of desserts—sometimes you get in a rut and forget what the possibilities are."

Shere says the ice creams and sherbets at Chez Panisse are especially popular.

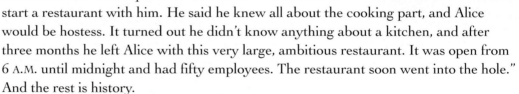

Her personal favorites are desserts made with fruit, because of the abundance available in California. "We make a lot of simple fruit dishes, soups with fruits, composed fruit things, and lots of crisps and casual desserts for the cafe."

Here Shere shares her recipes for a classic black bottom pie, some exquisite éclairs made with California's Meyer lemon, and a new kind of ice cream sandwich that's just plum delicious.

Black Bottom Pie

Serves 6-8

4	large eggs
1½	cups milk
2	ounces unsweetened chocolate
5	tablespoons packed light brown sugar
2	tablespoons plus 2 teaspoons all-purpose flour
3	tablespoons cognac
¼	teaspoon pure vanilla extract
1½	teaspoons gelatin
2	tablespoons cold water
¼	teaspoon cream of tartar
½	cup sugar, plus extra for whipped cream
1	9-inch pie shell, baked
1	cup whipping cream
1-2	tablespoons shaved unsweetened chocolate

A truly decadent dessert, this rich pie's "black bottom" is chocolate custard, topped by a cognac custard and whipped cream.

Separate eggs, reserving four yolks and three whites to come to room temperature.

In a small saucepan over high heat, scald milk.

In a double boiler, melt chocolate over warm water, and keep warm.

In a large, heavy saucepan, beat the four egg yolks, 3 tablespoons of the brown sugar, and all of the flour together. Gradually beat in the hot milk and cook over low heat until the mixture is thick (to 170° F), about 10 minutes. Remove from heat. Measure 1⅓ cups of this custard into a small bowl. Stir in the melted chocolate, the remaining 2 tablespoons brown sugar, 1 tablespoon of the cognac, and vanilla extract. Set aside to cool.

In a small saucepan, sprinkle gelatin over 2 tablespoons of cold water and soften for 5 minutes. Dissolve over low heat, stirring constantly. Stir gelatin into the reserved plain custard, with the remaining 2 tablespoons cognac, and set it over a bowl of ice water to cool, stirring constantly.

When the cognac custard has chilled to a syrupy consistency, about 5 minutes, beat the room-temperature egg whites with cream of tartar in a large bowl until they hold soft peaks. Gradually beat in ½ cup sugar until the whites hold stiff peaks. Fold in the cognac custard, taking care to scrape the bowl clean to use all the custard.

Spread chocolate custard in pie shell and spread the cognac custard over it.

Chill 2-3 hours or until the top is set.

Whip cream and sweeten to taste. Swirl decoratively over the top of the pie and sprinkle with shaved chocolate.

Meyer Lemon Éclairs

Makes 30 small éclairs

Most of the parts of this recipe may be made ahead, but the final assembly should be done within an hour or two of serving. Leftover éclair pastry may be frozen for later use.

FILLING

- 2 large eggs
- 3 egg yolks
- 6 tablespoons sugar
  Juice of 2 Meyer lemons (at least 6 ounces)
- 6 tablespoons unsalted butter
- ¼ teaspoon finely grated Meyer lemon zest

ÉCLAIRS

- 1 cup water
- 1 teaspoon sugar
- ⅛ teaspoon salt
- 6 tablespoons unsalted butter
- 1 cup all-purpose flour
- 4 or 5 large eggs

ASSEMBLY

- 1 cup sliced almonds
- 1 cup plus 2 teaspoons sugar
- 1 cup heavy cream
- ½ teaspoon pure vanilla extract

To make filling: In a small, heavy, non-reactive saucepan, whisk eggs and egg yolks until just mixed. Whisk in sugar and lemon juice.

Cut in the butter in small pieces. Add to mixture and cook over low heat, stirring constantly, until the mixture coats the spoon, 5-10 minutes. Remove from heat. If the mixture doesn't thicken on standing, return it to the heat and continue to cook a little longer.

Strain the mixture into a container and whisk in the grated zest. Refrigerate. *(The filling may be covered and refrigerated for 2-3 weeks.)*

To make éclairs: Preheat oven to 400° F.

Lightly grease baking sheets with butter and evenly dust with flour or line with parchment.

In a medium-size saucepan, bring water, sugar, salt, and butter to a boil. Remove from heat and quickly stir in flour. Return to the heat and cook until the mixture forms a ball and pulls away from the sides of the pan, about 5 min-

utes. Scrape into a large mixing bowl and let cool for 5 minutes.

Add 4 eggs to the dough one by one, beating after each addition, until the mixture looks satiny. It should hold a soft shape. If it seems too stiff, break the fifth egg into a bowl and stir it with a fork to break it up. Beat in bit by bit until the texture seems right.

Place the éclair mixture into a pastry bag fitted with a ¼-inch diameter round tip. Pipe strips about 2¾-inch long x ⅞-inch wide, an inch apart, onto the prepared baking sheets.

Reduce oven temperature to 375° F. Bake 20-25 minutes or until golden brown and crisp. Cool on a rack. Freeze immediately after cooling if desired.

To assemble: Reduce oven to 350° F. Place almonds in a pie plate and toast them in the oven for 5-7 minutes or until pale golden brown. Chop the almonds just enough to halve most of the slices.

Slice the reserved éclairs lengthwise in

half, reserving both pieces. Set aside.

Place a film of water on the bottom of a small, heavy pan. Add 1 cup of the sugar. Cook over medium heat until pale golden brown, about 5 minutes. Remove caramel from heat and cool slightly.

Dip the tops of the éclairs carefully into the caramel, keeping your fingers well away from it, and then roll the tops quickly in the toasted almonds. (Rewarm the caramel if necessary to insure a thin coating.) Set the tops aside to dry.

Whip cream, the remaining 2 teaspoons sugar, and vanilla until it can just barely be piped through a pastry bag.

Fill the bottom of each éclair with about 1½ teaspoons of the reserved lemon filling. Then pipe the whipped cream over the filling, using a ¼-inch diameter star tube. Pipe the cream in zigzags that slightly overlap the bottom edges so the cream will be visible when the top is put on.

Gingersnap Ice Cream Sandwiches with Plum Ice Cream

Makes 2½-3 dozen sandwiches

Here's a special version of the beloved ice cream sandwich—fresh plum ice cream with a spicy cookie on either side. These sandwiches can be made a week or two ahead of time. When it's time for a picnic, they can be packed with blue ice for traveling.

ço

GINGERSNAPS

- ¾ cup (1½ sticks) unsalted butter, room temperature
- ⅞ cup sugar, plus extra for sprinkling
- 1 large egg
- ¼ cup light molasses
- ½ teaspoon pure vanilla extract
- 2 cups all-purpose flour
- 1¾ teaspoons baking soda
- ½ teaspoon salt
- ¾ teaspoon cinnamon
- ¾ teaspoon ground ginger

ICE CREAM

- 1 pound tart-skinned plums, such as Santa Rosa, Casselman, Satsuma, Elephant Heart, or Mariposa
- 1 cup half-and-half
- 2 cups cream
- 1 cup sugar
- 6 egg yolks
- ¼ teaspoon pure vanilla extract, or to taste

To make gingersnaps: In a large mixing bowl, cream butter until light, add sugar and cream again until the mixture is light. Beat in egg, molasses, and vanilla.

In a small bowl, mix flour, baking soda, salt, cinnamon, and ginger. Sift if there are lumps in the baking soda. Be sure that your baking soda is fresh. Stir dry ingredients into the butter mixture. The dough will be soft.

Roll the dough into several rolls 1¾ inches in diameter, wrap in plastic wrap or parchment paper, and chill thoroughly. If the rolls have flattened, roll them back into shape again while they are cold enough to hold their shape. When chilled, put them in the freezer to harden.

Preheat oven to 350° F. Remove the rolls from freezer, let stand 5 minutes and cut into scant ¼-inch-thick slices. Lay the round cookies an inch apart on ungreased baking sheets, sprinkle the tops lightly with sugar and bake for 8-10 minutes or until the cookies have collapsed and are golden brown.

Cool on a rack; then freeze them flat on the baking sheet. They need to be frozen so they won't break easily when you assemble the sandwiches. They may then be put in a covered container and used later.

To make ice cream: Cut plums in half, remove pits, and cut into quarters. Place in a nonreactive saucepan over low heat with just enough water to cover the bottom of the pan. Cook, covered, until the skins are tender, 5-10 minutes. Puree in a blender or food processor. Measure out 1⅓ cups of the puree.

In a large nonreactive pan over high heat, scald cream, half-and-half, and sugar.

In a bowl, whisk egg yolks to break them up. Gradually whisk some of the hot cream mixture into the yolks.

Return mixture to the pan and cook over medium heat, stirring constantly, until the mixture coats the spoon, about 5 minutes. Stir in vanilla. Strain.

Stir in the reserved plum puree and chill.
Freeze according to the ice cream freezer manufacturer's directions.

To assemble: Turn half of the ginger-snaps bottom-side-up. Scoop about 2 tablespoons of the ice cream onto each bottom-side-up gingersnap. Let soften briefly. Cover with the remaining gingersnaps, and press on top, pushing the ice cream to the edge of the cookie. Return to the freezer on baking sheets to harden. Wrap each one in plastic wrap or wax paper to store.

Jody Adams • A Contemporary Italian Dinner • page 168

The pasta and salmon need wines with crisp acidity and forward fruit. Choose a sparkling wine from Roederer Estate or Scharffenberger, or a stylish blend of Sauvignon Blanc/Sémillon. These wines could also be paired to the chicken, or choose a supple, juicy red, such as Beringer's Gamay Beaujolais, or a grenache from Bonny Doon.

Monique Barbeau • Pacific Northwest Bounty • page 34

Full-flavored seafood dishes with tangy, spicy, and herbal components call for a rich white wine with crisp acidity and citrus and herb-tinged flavors. Excellent choices to go through this menu would be a Sauvignon Blanc/Sémillon blend from Matanzas Creek or Merryvale.

Lidia Bastianich • Italian Border Cuisine • page 94

A fine complement to the soup and the swordfish would be a crisp and fruity white wine of medium body. Choose Ferrari-Carano's Fumé Blanc or the Rodney Strong "Charlotte's Home Vineyard" Sauvignon Blanc. The rigatoni needs a red wine with depth to not get lost in the lusty flavors of the sauce. Try a Zinfandel from Frog's Leap or Beringer.

Catherine Brandel • Napa Valley Harvest • page 64

In keeping with the Italian flavors of the salad, try a brisk Pinot Gris from Oregon. The best producers include Eyrie and Argyle. With the gnocchi and wild mushrooms, look for a ripe and creamy Chardonnay with subtle shadings of earth and spice. Beautiful wines in this style come from Chalone and Kistler. Grilled pigeon is ideal for the smooth cherry/berry flavors and warm spice of a fine Pinot Noir. Try one of the excellent bottlings from Carneros Creek or Rex Hill.

Kathy Cary • Southern Progressive Fare • page 40

Pair the blini with one of California's many outstanding sparkling wines, such as Roederer Estate or Scharffenberger. You might also enjoy a medium-bodied Sauvignon Blanc/Sémillon blend from Vichon or Lakewood, either of which would pair well with the spinach tart. The creamy, apple-y flavors of the scallops call for a full-bodied Chardonnay. Choose Grgich Hills or De Loach.

Traci Des Jardins • Contemporary French Cuisine • page 10

For the tuna choose a bright and juicy Russian River Valley Pinot Noir with some mild earthy nuances, such as Rodney Strong or Rochioli. Choose a crisp but fairly rich Sauvignon Blanc/Sémillon blend for the scallops. I suggest Kalin and Lockwood. For the duck, a Zinfandel from Niebaum-Coppola, or a ripe, smooth Pinot Noir from Cambria or Morgan.

Nancy Flume • Seattle Seafood Sublime • page 130

The complex of bright and spicy flavors in this menu, with its appealing mix of subtle heat and fresh herbs, calls for an equally vibrant white

wine with clear and direct flavors. I like the blends of Sauvignon Blanc and Sémillon from Matanzas Creek and Merryvale, but a bottle of bubbly from Piper-Sonoma or Argyle would also be a terrific match.

Gale Gand • A Simple Savory Supper • page 100

The creamy-textured soup with its subtle interplay of sweet and toasty flavors make it a good match for a Chardonnay from Arrowood or Beringer. You might choose to continue with the Chardonnay into the salmon course. A Pinot Noir would also be a lovely way to accent the earthy elements in this dish. Choose Acacia or Saintsbury.

Elka Gilmore • Pacific Rim Elegance • page 156

Celebrate the vivid flavors of the elegant seafood with a sparkling wine. The extra dimensions of fruit and spice of a Blanc de Noirs would be the top choice. Look for Mumm Napa Valley or Domaine Chandon. With the lobster try an equally rich, full-flavored white wine. A Chardonnay from Bernardus or Swanson would prove memorable.

Joyce Goldstein • A Tempting Mediterranean Menu • page 124

A lean and tangy Sauvignon Blanc makes the best partner for the asparagus as well as the roasted pepper salad. Try a bottle from Rochioli, Duckhorn, or St. Clement. For the lamb, try one of California's many excellent Cabernet Sauvignons. Laurel Glen, Spotteswood, and Shafer are all superb.

Deborah Hughes • Innovative Northern Italian • page 52

An ideal choice for the gazpacho would be a Sauvignon Blanc from Simi, Buena Vista, or Rochioli. For the duck salad and grilled steak, look for an assertive red with a sweet core of fruit and some peppery, smoky nuances. Choose a Zinfandel from Ridge Vineyard—Geyserville or Lytton Springs bottlings. A Syrah from Swanson or Edmunds St. John would also be a great match.

Raji Jallepalli • French-Indian Fusion • page 88

The lively flavors in the two seafood dishes are best paired to a crisp white wine with herbal and citrus notes. Choose a Sauvignon Blanc from De Loach or Flora Springs. For the pork, try a silky Pinot Noir with sweet/tart cherry flavors and mild earth and spice notes. Top producers include Au Bon Climat, Acacia, and Saintsbury.

Donna Katzl • A Cozy Midwinter Supper • page 162

A medium-bodied Zinfandel with bright and peppery berry flavors is my choice for the gorgonzola toasts and the lamb orzotto in this menu. Top producers include Quivira and Kenwood.

Katy Keck • East Meets Southwest • page 22

Good picks for both the shrimp and the Asian salad include vibrantly fruity, crisply acidic wines like Blanc de Noirs from Maison Deutz,

Mumm Napa Valley or Domaine Chandon. For the pork, try a juicy red—a Grenache from Bonny Doon or a Dolcetto from Rasmussen.

Johanne Killeen • Trattoria Tastes • page 118
The sweet earthiness of caramelized onions, turnips, and apples combined with the cream suggests a smooth Chardonnay with gentle spice. Look for wines from La Crema and Morgan. The spaghettini goes well with a tart and fruity Italian red wine. An excellent choice from California is the Barbera from Louis M. Martini. Try a Sangiovese from Atlas Peak or Swanson with the roasted sausages.

Mary Sue Milliken & Susan Feniger • Greek Revival • page 142
The tangy, vibrant flavors of this Mediterranean-inspired menu call for crisp wines with bright fruit flavors. A Blanc de Noirs sparkling wine from Mumm Napa Valley or Maison Deutz would be a good choice, as would an assertive Sauvignon Blanc from Kenwood or Morgan.

Cindy Pawlcyn • A Tapas Evening • page 82
Stick with a crisp and fruity dry white wine for this entire meal of little bites. Try a Fumé Blanc from Ferrari-Carano or a Sauvignon Blanc from R.H. Phillips or Clos Du Bois.

Debra Ponzek • Provençal Inspirations • page 58
Luxurious and silky smooth, this soup calls for a similarly styled white wine of some depth. Chardonnays from Chalone and Kistler or a Pinot Blanc from Chalone are all excellent choices, and would also pair nicely with the cod.

Odessa Piper • Heartland Magic • page 150
Begin with a light, crisp sparkling wine from Domaine Carneros or Cordorniu Napa. Each would allow the purity of flavors in the tuna to shine through. With the subtle flavors of the soup, try a light-bodied Pinot Noir from Au Bon Climat or Sanford. California is producing some stunning red wines from syrah grapes that would pair well with the venison. Top producers include Edmunds St. John and Swanson.

Nora Pouillon • An Elegant Spring Dinner • page 16
Sautéed morels and goat cheese have a woodsy, earthy dimension akin to that of the grilled salmon, while each dish is perked up by a tart component like the beet vinaigrette or the lemongrass. This points to light-bodied Pinot Noir with similar components or a Blanc de Noirs sparkling wine. Try a Pinot Noir from Acacia or Saintsbury or a Blanc de Noirs from Mumm, Napa Valley, or Maison Deutz.

Patty Queen • Winter Warmth • page 106
With the ravioli, try a full-bodied Blanc de Noirs from Mumm Napa Valley, or a sparkling rosé from Domaine Chandon. The creamy bisque suggests a smooth, rich Chardonnay. Excellent producers include Bernardus and Swanson. To complement the pork loin, try a Pinot Noir with bright red berry flavors, such as Acacia or Saintsbury. If you prefer a white wine, look for Gewürztraminer from Navarro or De Loach.

Anne Rosenzweig • Notable New York • page 136
For the ravioli, try a Chardonnay from Swanson or J. Stonestreet. Both wines are lush and smooth, with rich fruit flavors and toasty oak nuances. With the chicken, try a lively Blanc de Noirs sparkling wine from Mumm Napa Valley or Maison Deutz, or a rosé from Joseph Phelps–great choices for the sweet-tart complexities of this vibrant dish.

Teresa Rovito • A Night in Milan • page 28
The bruschetta, carpaccio, and risotto have flavors that are tangy, salty, herbal, and creamy. My choice would be a medium-bodied white wine with well-defined structure and refreshing acidity. Sparkling wines from Mumm Napa Valley, Roederer Estate, or Scharffenberger would make great choices, as would the Sauvignon Blanc/Sémillon blends from Matanzas Creek and Vichon. With the chicken in red wine—a Pinot Noir from Mondavi or Etude.

RoxSand Scocos • Tantalizing Fusion Cuisine • page 174
Tender white rabbit loin, creamy polenta, and sweet roasted peppers are ideal with the smooth and focused flavors of a balanced Chardonnay from Acacia, Au Bon Climat, or Morgan. A Pinot Noir from any one of these producers would work wonders with the shiitake risotto.

Peggy Smith • Salute to Summer • page 112
With the corn soup and the salad, look for a Sauvignon Blanc/Sémillon blend from Matanzas Creek or Vichon. These wines have the texture and weight to balance these dishes and the right amount of fruit intensity and acidity for the tomatoes, herbs, and vinaigrette. You could continue with these wines for the lobster salad, but an even better match would be a Chardonnay. Try Acacia or Argyle.

Susan Spicer • Global Gourmet • page 70
The spicy, aromatic flavors of this soup are ideal with a rosé. Fine examples come from Bonny Doon and Joseph Phelps. The more intense flavors of the salad and shrimp would pair very nicely with a Sauvignon Blanc from Dry Creek or Kunde. Both wines complement the herbal components of these dishes and provide refreshing contrast.

Sarah Stegner • A Chilled Late-Summer Menu • page 46
For a wine with the marinated roasted peppers, choose one that's light and crisp, like a Sauvignon Blanc from Robert Pepi or Spotteswoode. With the salmon, try a lively and sweetly perfumed Gewürztraminer from California's Anderson Valley. Look for Handley or Navarro.

Elizabeth Terry • Southern Comfort Cooking • page 76
The salad calls for a fruity, smooth white wine with good acidity that's not too sharp. Choose a Fumé Blanc from Ferrari-Carano or a Sémillon from Chateau Ste. Michelle. Roasted game hens are a fine pairing for medium-weight Chardonnays with good focus and lighter-bodied Pinot Noirs for those who prefer a red. I recommend a Central Coast Chardonnay from Meridian or Au Bon Climat. Compatible Pinot Noirs include those from Saintsbury and Sanford.

Index

Metric Conversion Guidelines

These guidelines were developed to simplify the conversion from Imperial measures to metric. The numbers have been rounded for convenience. When cooking from a recipe, work in the same system throughout, do not use a combination of the two.

LIQUID MEASURES

Imperial	Metric
¼ teaspoon	1 milliliter (ml)
½ teaspoon	2 ml
¾ teaspoon	4 ml
1 teaspoon	5 ml
2 teaspoons	10 ml
1 tablespoon	15 ml
2 tablespoons	25 ml
¼ cup	50 ml
⅓ cup	75 ml
½ cup	125 ml
⅔ cup	150 ml
¾ cup	175 ml
1 cup	250 ml
2 cups	500 ml
4 cups	1 liter
5 cups	1.25 liters

SOLID MEASURES

Imperial	Metric
1 ounce	25 grams
2 ounces	50 grams
¼ pound	125 grams
½ pound	250 grams
1 pound	500 grams
2 pounds	1 kilogram
3 pounds	1.5 kilograms
5 pounds	2.2 kilograms

LENGTH

Imperial	Metric
¼ inch	5 millimeters (mm)
⅓ inch	8 mm
½ inch	1 centimeter (cm)
¾ inch	2 cm
1 inch	2.5 cm
2 inches	5 cm
4 inches	10 cm

OVEN TEMPERATURE CONVERSIONS

Imperial	Metric
250° Fahrenheit (F)	120° Celsius (C)
275° F	140° C
300° F	150° C
325° F	160° C
350° F	180° C
375° F	190° C
400° F	200° C
425° F	220° C
450° F	230° C
500° F	260° C